After spending several years working on trying to retain people from welfare in manufacturing jobs at Cascade Engineering, it was Phil DeVol's insights that made the difference. We learned that not only did we need to understand our welfare employees' life situations, we needed to change from judging their actions to meeting their needs. Not only did we succeed in retaining our welfare employees, we improved our overall culture and support for all employees. We call our program "Welfare to Career" because people stay for our lifestyle, not just a job.

> **–Fred Keller,** Chairman and CEO
> Cascade Engineering
> Grand Rapids, Michigan

The presentations by Ruby Payne in May 2008 in Slovakia and the later visit by Phil DeVol in the fall of that year in Kosice, Slovakia, brought about deep, positive changes in thinking among both lay workers and professionals in understanding causes of poverty. We learned a healing philosophy that builds cooperation among all social classes in communities and society. One of the results of these changes is that the city government of Kosice (population 250,000) endorsed the concepts of the Bridges Out of Poverty book as a strategy for dealing with poverty. My organization, The Council for Advising in Social Work, was entrusted with preparing a comprehensive application of Phil and Ruby's know-how. We have introduced a methodology of "Crossing Bridges" to this city and to the neighboring city of Presov (population 100,000). We want to thank the people at aha! Process, Inc. for their trust and willingness to work with us. We believe that together we will create the pathway toward our desired goals.

> **–Judita Varcholova,** Director
> The Council for Advising in Social Work
> Kosice, Slovakia

I have consistently relied on the Bridges Out of Poverty training that I was fortunate to receive as a state trial court judge in operating a drug court docket. The Bridges curriculum was the catalyst that guided the concepts and creation of "Better Lives, Better Ohio," a web-based social health index to help Ohio achieve greater economic and social prosperity.

The Bridges concepts work at the individual, community, and state levels. I have seen this in action as many individuals rise from poverty, better understanding the resources they have and how to obtain them from their communities. Those helped by Bridges often become motivated to give back to their communities. Our communities benefit from the integration and participation of many, reflecting the true spirit of democracy.

Bridges concepts help restore the vigor of the American dream so that individuals from all walks of life can imagine and write their own future stories. Bridges to Sustainable Communities is a needed next step in helping our communities do the same.

–**Jennifer Brunner,** Secretary of State
State of Ohio

We have been doing a lot to help people live in poverty—but not a lot to help people get out of it. We all have to do something to change that.

–**Alivia Douglas,** Student Volunteer
Corcoran High School
Syracuse, New York

The Bridges Out of Poverty approach is significant because it gives us a road map out of the entrenched problem of poverty while providing for autonomy in the way each community chooses to operationalize the concepts. It is built on participatory and democratic notions that it will take all economic classes to solve the problem of poverty, all sectors, all faiths, all political persuasions.

As we employ Bridges in our community, we are finding new collaborations, new energy, and renewed hope. We network with the other communities like ours, whether in Ohio or Slovakia, to share ideas and best practices. We connect with similar initiatives to find ways to anchor and expand the effort. In the middle of it all, Phil DeVol champions the work, encouraging us, feeding us new research and ideas, and helping us build a sustainable movement to end poverty in our lifetime. I feel like we are doing our small but important piece to work toward a prosperous community, nation, and planet.

–**Bonnie Bazata,** Executive Director
St. Joseph County Bridges Out of Poverty Initiative
South Bend, Indiana

The Bridges Out of Poverty program in South Bend and St. Joseph County has served as a catalyst to bring together social service agencies, government, institutions and businesses to form partnerships that we had envisioned but never before achieved. People with different backgrounds and political leanings found common ground and mission. Most importantly, individuals who have experienced generational poverty are enriching the discussion as we learn from each other. This is critical to the success of the initiative. One of the aspects of Bridges Out of Poverty that I find most effective is the feedback loops that allow for continual review and improvement. This book shows the growth and refinement of the Bridges effort, which has kept it fresh and effective.

–Stephen J. Luecke, Mayor
South Bend, Indiana

For more than 20 years I have committed personal and professional time and talents to education, human services, youth development, probation, alternative dispute resolution, and ending-racism work within my community. It wasn't until I read and applied Bridges Out of Poverty concepts and strategies—and partnered with people from varying races, classes, and abilities—that it all came together for me. This is about a sustainable community for all, not just some. How you supervise, manage, engage, volunteer, support, and empower people is influenced heavily by the economic class you were raised in. Who are we to believe that the "old" way of doing things make sense for everyone? We are all worthy of economic stability and life prosperity. The challenge is: What are we willing to do about it? Everything starts with having new eyes!

–Angela M. Douglas, Campaign Director
Visions For Change, Inc.
Bridges Certified Trainer and Getting Ahead Facilitator
Syracuse, New York

Through my work with Habitat for Humanity, I have never come across a more comprehensive curriculum that goes ... beyond informing and teaching individuals. We use this curriculum to empower community volunteers to partner with our families who are on a journey out of poverty. This model allows our community to partner with our families to transform their lives. Every Habitat affiliate should incorporate this powerful tool into its family process.

–Clinton Moore, Director of Family Services
Flatirons Habitat for Humanity
Boulder, Colorado

One of the important mental models for me has been the research on the four areas of poverty. This research isn't based on just one area—the choices of individuals in poverty—but it also includes the absence of human and social capital in our communities, as well as exploitation and political/economic structures. There is a shift in thought for the participants who work with the Getting Ahead workbook when they realize they aren't solely responsible for their poverty. This becomes a bridge for them to believe that if a community works together to eliminate all these causes of poverty, there is hope for a sustainable community.

> **–Lindora Cabral,** RSM, Sister of Mercy
> Mercy Connections, Inc.
> Burlington, Vermont

In 15-plus years of working in human resources, I heard every excuse why an employee could not make it to work. In 2006 I read Bridges Out of Poverty and it changed my judgmental attitude toward those employees on the lower rungs of the economic ladder. Today I lead an organization that works with businesses and the community, using the hidden rules and Bridges constructs, to change the conversation and mindsets surrounding individuals in and around poverty.

> **–Jerry Mainstone,** Executive Director
> BC CAREERS
> Battle Creek, Michigan

This process provides encouragement, self-esteem, motivation, and belief that you can really get out of poverty. It's more than just talking about it. This [program] was the push to make it happen. This is a new family that gives me the strength to continue.

> **–Louise Randell,** Contact Community Services
> 2007 Getting Ahead Graduate
> Syracuse, New York

Thank you for all you have written. We are all indebted to you for the legacy of your writing that continues to guide our work daily.

> **–David Campbell,** Chief of Staff
> Community Properties of Ohio
> Columbus, Ohio

One of the most unique and significant aspects of Bridges has been its applicability to my own life as a person who crossed the bridge out of poverty. Exposure to Bridges gave me a language and context for my own life experiences, which now helps me better serve disenfranchised groups of people and helps me guide my staff as they train others within our organization and throughout communities statewide. I consistently see "ahas!" when Bridges concepts sink into the minds of groups of folks with whom I share, train, teach, and counsel, including people with a full range of developmental/intellectual, acquired, physical, emotional, sensory, and mobility disabilities, as well as addicts, alcoholics, young people, and couples.

Bridges helps teachers at all levels better understand and deal with students and helps people in the full range of helping professions understand and better serve clients. I have also experienced how the concepts help lawmakers and policy makers better understand the people they serve and results in creation of better laws. Bridges is not a solution, but it is solution-focused— and its principles provide a solid pathway to help people understand, factor through, and create change in their lives.

–**Dave Schaad,** Project Director/Assistant Lecturer
University of Wyoming/Wyoming Institute for Disabilities
Cheyenne, Wyoming

BRIDGES TO SUSTAINABLE COMMUNITIES

A SYSTEMWIDE, CRADLE-TO-GRAVE APPROACH TO ENDING POVERTY IN AMERICA

Bridges to Sustainable Communities: A Systemwide, Cradle-to-Grave
   Approach to Ending Poverty in America
Copyright 2010 by Philip E. DeVol.
   Second edition: 2015
   240 pp.

aha! Process, Inc.
P.O. Box 727
Highlands, TX 77562-0727
(800) 424-9484 ▪ (281) 426-5300
Fax: (281) 426-5600
Website: www.ahaprocess.com

Copy editing by Dan Shenk
Book and cover design by Frieda Probst

ISBN: 978-1-938248-69-6

EDITOR'S NOTE: The papers that comprise this book were
produced over a period of five years. Just as language changes and
evolves, so does the style of written communication. Therefore,
between/among the chapters the reader can expect to find some
differences in how like material is presented, but each chapter is
intended to be internally consistent.

BRIDGES TO SUSTAINABLE COMMUNITIES

**A SYSTEMWIDE,
CRADLE-TO-GRAVE APPROACH
TO ENDING POVERTY
IN AMERICA**

Philip E. DeVol

■ ■ ■ ■

Dedication

This collection of writings is largely the result of ideas and insights triggered by great conversations and activities with people who have been part of the Bridges community of practice the past decade. Thanks for all you've done to advance the work and for making our communities better places to live.

TABLE OF CONTENTS
ANNOTATED

This paper brings together core aha! Process concepts with new information and tools that have been developed in the last 10 years. It provides an overview of Bridges constructs with a focus on community-level action.

Here we cover the theory and design of *Getting Ahead,* the workbook that helps people investigate the impact that poverty has had on them and their communities. It brings people in poverty into the planning and decision-making process at the community level.

This paper describes how problems get named and the mindsets behind different approaches to change. It introduces the positive, but realistic, approach that aha! Process takes to poverty issues, contrasting it with the deficit model.

Disasters often happen quickly and dramatically, but sometimes they creep up on a community. This paper is a quick guide to how aha! Process can help in both cases.

Part I of this paper is a quick read—a summary of foundational books, processes, and features of the Bridges Model.

Part II is for communities that have made a decision to organize themselves around Bridges constructs. Learning from communities that lead the way, it lays out guiding and organizing principles, as well as step-by-step instructions.

This paper challenges Bridges Steering Committees to play a larger role in their communities. It introduces the Bridges Continuum, a tool for the development of comprehensive cradle-to-grave strategies that can be used to attract people from all sectors to the work of creating prosperous communities. Bridges Steering Committees are encouraged to do whole system planning, to operate above the "silos," and to focus on metrics that really matter.

Bridges is not a program. It is a set of constructs, ideas, strategies, and best practices. It also offers a number of tools to help innovators apply the ideas in their organizations and communities. The 12 thinking tools found here help planners move from the abstract concepts to action.

An insight is a restructuring of information; it's seeing the same old thing in a completely new way. Once that restructuring occurs, you never go back.

–Earl Miller
Massachusetts Institute of Technology
"The Eureka Hunt" by Jonah Lehrer, *The New Yorker*, July 28, 2008

■ ■ ■ ■

Introduction

If ever there was a time that people needed new ways
to talk with each other about poverty, prosperity, and
community sustainability, this is it. In the wake of the "Great
Economic Meltdown of 2008," communities are being challenged to
remain or, in some cases, become socially and economically viable.

This six-part book provides a new way of talking and doing based
on a foundation of terms, constructs, models, and strategies that a
number of communities are using to address poverty and prosperity
in comprehensive ways. This collection of papers arises from *Bridges
Out of Poverty*, which was written by Dr. Ruby K. Payne, Terie Dreussi
Smith, and me in 1999. People who had read *Bridges* and attended
workshops by that name began to self-organize to create communities that worked on poverty issues in new and creative ways.
Since 2001 "Bridges Communities" have sprung up in the United
States, Canada, Australia, and Slovakia. These papers chart the
changes and development in Bridges work since 2001.

My primary purpose in publishing this compilation of papers is to
help struggling communities pass on a high quality of life to the next
generation. I also want to encourage existing Bridges Communities
to respond to the challenges posed by the Great Economic Meltdown. These papers can be taken selectively to fill in gaps—or as a
whole to inform people who are new to our work. I think of these
papers as an overview of ideas that are foundational to individual,
organizational, and community change. Creative people have taken

our ideas, added them to their own best practices, and developed programs and applications that already have delivered amazing results. Some of these stories appear on our website (www.bridges outofpoverty.com). Readers should know that Bridges Communities are active; we do, we learn, and we pass it on. Our community of practice is growing.

Bridges Communities have a working knowledge of poverty that can help those who have been impacted by the economic crisis. With a recent job-loss rate of 600,000 a month, many people will be driven into the "tyranny of the moment," a feature of poverty that people who were already living in the rubble at the bottom of the economy are familiar with. Finding a place to stay, gas for the car, and food for the kids demands immediate, concrete solutions. In a shaky world, whether it's due to a recent foreclosure or to persistent poverty, it's tougher and takes longer to solve daily living problems. Instability robs people of their future orientation, their ability to resist predators (who provide concrete solutions at inflated costs), and the time they need to investigate solutions that will get them into a stable environment.

But it isn't just people in poverty who experience the tyranny of the moment, it's civilian populations in war, it's victims of natural disasters, it's organizations whose budgets have been slashed, and it's cities and counties that have lost their tax base. The National League of Cities survey showed that 84% of U.S. cities recently report facing fiscal difficulties. Some 92% expected to have trouble meeting their city's needs the remainder of this year, 69% have instituted hiring freezes or layoffs, 42% were delaying or canceling infrastructure projects, and 22% have instituted across-the-board cuts. Cities' tax revenues are declining as property values drop, shopping slows, and unemployment rises.

The sudden economic collapse masks the already existing downward trend that underlies the problem. U.S. cities have been in decline since 1970. Using three objective indices of urban life—poverty rates, unemployment rates, and real per capita incomes changes—just three cities in 1970 were in trouble with a normalized index more than 30% higher than the national average. In 1980, fully 20 cities were having difficulty by the same measure. In a study that captured data prior to the financial upheaval in September 2008, Moody's Economy reported that two-thirds of this nation's 381 metropolitan areas were in recession, and another one in five was at risk.

The point is that the problems our communities are facing today have been building for a long time. Families in poverty and those of us doing Bridges work knew that many communities were in trouble. The problems only came to light in a significant way in September 2008. In fact, our communities are in as much difficulty as the families who live in them. Now many U.S. cities are in poverty. The toll that poverty takes on individuals and families is increasingly being felt by community leaders and our communities in general.

We cannot allow the old and dead ideas that brought our communities to this point to be the answers for the future. We can't get through this recession by trying to get back to the way we were. "The way we were" contributed to these problems. There are forces afoot that are deeper than the present crisis—factors that transcend the current difficulties. For example, globalization as we know it isn't working very well for those of us in the West. While globalization narrowed the income and wealth gap between the rich nations and the poor nations, the income and wealth gap between the rich and the poor in the United States was widening. Of the 30 nations in the Organization for Economic Cooperation and Development, the U.S. was already the third highest in income disparity, just behind Mexico and Turkey.

The old and dead ideas on how to build prosperous communities won't work either. We used to create wealth by manufacturing products like steel and cars. Then we convinced ourselves that we could let go of making physical products and, instead, create wealth by devising financial products around loans, mortgages, and fees.

These factors, among others, resulted in a downward pressure on wages that is very likely to extend beyond the recovery period for this recession and into the future. Well-paying jobs are at the heart of establishing economic stability. In Bridges Communities we know that to talk about poverty we also must talk about wealth-creating mechanisms.

The federal, state, and local strategies for getting people out of poverty before the economic downturn weren't working; in fact, the number of people in persistent and concentrated poverty was on the rise. Those piecemeal approaches to alleviating and preventing poverty didn't even have an intention of getting people out of poverty—only of getting people off public assistance. And now, due to the Great Economic Meltdown, there are even more people in poverty and more people out of work—plus it's becoming that much harder for people at the bottom to make the transition out of poverty. The old and dead ideas for getting people out of poverty won't do.

The Great Economic Meltdown did one good thing: It blew away the myths that all was well, that things were working, that with a little more hard work and "pulling themselves up by their own boot-straps" people would get out of poverty, that every entity doing its part would lead to the good life, that a little tweaking of the system would set everything right again.

Keeping in mind that each crisis brings with it opportunities for new approaches and positive changes, Bridges Communities have the knowledge base, principles, strategies, tools, and partners to develop innovative solutions. With our lengthening Bridges track record, we know how to avoid getting stuck in the tyranny of the moment and how to build a future story in the midst of chaos.

We would like to help other communities lay the foundation for high-impact and comprehensive strategies of their own. Through the Texas-based aha! Process organization (Dr. Ruby Payne's company, which provides products and training for those working with people in poverty), we worked with many different catalysts and visionaries to help fuel and accelerate the work of Bridges Communities.We worked with the business community and found that the private sector could use the foundation we laid to quickly get good results with new hires from poverty. And we found a way to engage people in poverty, bringing them to the planning table to help solve community problems.

The papers compiled in this book tell the story of the development of the Bridges methodology and process. They point to how the Bridges Communities model can help neighborhoods and communities build a future where everyone can do well. This collection of papers includes a synopsis of the book *Bridges Out of Poverty*, explains how to engage people from all classes and sectors, expands on core concepts, describes how aha! Process and the community can respond to natural disasters and persistent poverty, illustrates how Bridges Communities are formed, and provides tools for Bridges Steering Committees.

These papers can help the reader in three ways: (1) They serve as "CliffsNotes"for the foundational ideas that come from *Bridges Out of Poverty*; (2) they describe new models, ideas, applications, and tools that we have developed as communities took ownership of the work; and (3) they present guidelines and action steps for the future.

The *first paper,* *"Using the Hidden Rules of Class to Create Sustainable Communities,"* describes and expands on the core constructs found in *Bridges Out of Poverty.* It offers accurate descriptions (mental models) of the living environments of poverty, middle class, and wealth. It holds up the lens of economic class as a way of analyzing the complexities of poverty. It also provides the community with a shared language with which to address both poverty and prosperity issues. This lexicon includes a:

- Definition of poverty that is much more than a simple income guideline.

- Description of the hidden rules of class to help us develop relationships of mutual respect.

5

- Review of the research on the causes of poverty so that we can become proficient at addressing all the causes, not just one or two.

The paper defines a community that is at risk—and suggests an accountability tool for communities, as well as principles for change.

We have learned much from people, communities, and organizations that already have applied Bridges concepts. Our work has been used by numerous neighborhoods and communities, including those that are largely African American, Native American, Appalachian, Caucasian, Hispanic/Latino, urban, and rural. People in poverty have informed and helped develop our books and strategies. They have used the workbook *Getting Ahead in a Just-Gettin'-By World* to examine the impact that poverty has on them and their communities. Getting Ahead engages people in poverty as problem solvers, as vital members of planning and decision-making groups. The **second paper,** *"Getting Ahead Philosophy and Process,"* describes the philosophy and process for the Getting Ahead work-group experience.

The **third paper,** *"Additive Model: aha! Process's Approach to Building Sustainable Communities,"* outlines the additive model used by aha! Process. In it we challenge the "chicken inspector" mindset of the deficit model and discuss the danger of not taking a comprehensive approach and, as a result, ending up blaming the individual. The additive model recognizes what people from all classes bring to the table and advocates for shared decision making. Community members are encouraged to see themselves as "barn raisers" rather than "consumers at vending machines."

The paper on disaster recovery is particularly pertinent given the economic crisis of 2008 and 2009. When circumstances force us into survival mode, we can get trapped in the tyranny of the moment where we can't see beyond next week—or even tomorrow—because we're busy solving immediate, concrete problems. So it is that the very strategies and skills needed to survive during wars, natural disasters, and persistent poverty are the very things that make us vulnerable to predators. Exploiting the vulnerable is easy if the service or product meets a tangible need and is delivered by those who feign concern and respect. Communities also can get stuck in the tyranny of the moment just as individuals can. The *fourth paper, "Disaster Recovery Plan,"* is a quick read on how to respond to disasters.

The *fifth paper, "Building Bridges Communities,"* describes how Bridges Communities were formed. It is a description, not a prescription. Every community has its unique history, population, leadership, circumstances, and approaches. Taking ownership of the Bridges constructs is the first step. This leads to self-organizing and taking action. The paper offers lessons learned from other communities; it also describes the role of the Bridges Steering Committee, guiding principles, start-up steps, strategies, and supports that are available.

The *sixth paper, "Whole System Planning,"* introduces the Bridges Continuum, a tool for BSCs. The continuum can assist in bringing all sectors and demographics to the table:

- The service and health sectors to help stabilize an unstable environment

- Education to prepare individuals to pursue their dreams

- The business sector to help people acquire income, assets, and wealth

The continuum covers poverty from cradle to grave and also provides for a balanced life and prosperous community. Poverty is typically addressed from the heart, from the moral and social justice perspective. This paper addresses poverty from the head as well, by providing metrics and fallout costs—and showing the benefits that each sector of the community derives from the work of the others. The business sector, for example, can see that early-childhood interventions can have a return of 15 to 17% on dollars spent by helping prepare children to learn. The sixth paper advocates for whole system planning and describes the role of Bridges partners and champions.

Readers unfamiliar with Bridges will want to read the first paper to learn Bridges core concepts before moving on. People already familiar with Bridges constructs, such as those who have attended our workshops or are serving on a Bridges Steering Committee, may choose to move directly to the paper that most interests them.

The *seventh paper,* "12 Thinking Tools," is primarily designed for people who want to make changes at the institutional and community levels. Again, it assumes that the reader is familiar with Bridges concepts as found in *Bridges Out of Poverty, Getting Ahead in a Just-Gettin'-By World,* and the first paper in this book. Each thinking tool is described briefly using a simple pattern: (a) the problem statement, (b) a mental model representing the tool, (c) the context in which the tool is applied, (d) the core ideas, (e) ways to use the tool with brief examples, and (f) information on where to learn more.

Finally, a cautionary note. At the beginning of this piece I quoted Earl Miller of M.I.T.: "An insight is a restructuring of information; it's seeing the same old thing in a completely new way. Once that restructuring occurs, you never go back." Somewhere in these papers you might have had an insight or two. If that has occurred, I want you to know—you can never go back!

■ ■ ■ ■

■ ■ ■ ■

The way children experience life is determined by the families and communities in which they are raised; it falls to families and communities to create a way of life that is healthy, prosperous, and sustainable.

In her seminal 1996 work A Framework for Understanding Poverty *(third revised edition, 2003), Dr. Ruby K. Payne introduces the concept of hidden rules of economic class—and in future works she addresses sustainability, the next major challenge all communities must face. With Payne's ideas as a springboard, this paper seeks to contribute to the dialogue.*

Economic and social trends going back to the 1970s show a decline in the quality of life in the United States. The middle class is shrinking (Lind 2004, pp. 120-128), social connectedness is declining in all social classes (Putnam 2000, pp. 9, 63), some rural areas are losing population and the sense of community they once had (Lind 2003, pp. 86-88), some urban areas are collapsing as middle-class families move to the suburbs looking for good schools (Warren 2003, p. 8), and working a second job is required to make ends meet (Miringoff 2000, p. 9). For low-wage workers, vulnerability is becoming a concrete experience; for people in generational poverty, vulnerability has always been a concrete experience.

This paper addresses the impact of generational poverty on families and communities, why we must respond, and how to use an understanding of economic diversity to build sustainable communities.

THE SEQUENCE INCLUDES:
- *Creating a mental model of poverty and middle class.*
- *Exploring the hidden rules of economic class that arise from those experiences.*
- *Examining the resources that define quality of life.*
- *Creating a mental model of communities at risk.*
- *Reviewing poverty research to uncover strategies for change.*
- *Naming the barriers to change for people in poverty.*
- *Defining strategies for change based on the research.*
- *Exploring evaluations and reports used to monitor progress.*
- *Defining the principles for change.*
- *Outlining community roles for creating sustainable communities.*
- *Offering a mental model for prosperity.*

–Philip E. DeVol

1

USING THE HIDDEN RULES OF CLASS
TO CREATE SUSTAINABLE COMMUNITIES

First published for the State of Wyoming in 2004

PARTICIPATING IN COMMUNITY CHANGE

Peter Senge, author of *The Fifth Discipline*, provides
three definitions that can assist any group of people
entering into a change process together. He defines a
dialogue as a conversation that opens up a topic, examines facts,
explores meaning, and promotes understanding. A *discussion* takes
place when the group wants to narrow down the thinking and work
toward a decision. Both are necessary to the process.

Senge defines *mental models* as internal pictures of how the world
works or, in this case, how families function, what poverty is, and
how communities can solve problems (Senge 1994, pp. 174-204).

It is important also to define the term "community." For the purpose
of this paper, the definition provided by Daniel Taylor-Ide and Carl
Taylor in their book *Just and Lasting Change* will be used. They define
community as "… any group that has something in common and
the potential for acting together" (Taylor-Ide 2002, p. 19).

Members of a community who participate in a dialogue on community
sustainability will need to be willing to suspend their existing mental
models. Genuine dialogue cannot take place if individuals cling to
their own mental models to the extent that ideas expressed by others
are judged, categorized, and discarded as soon as they have been
stated. There are many mental models of poverty. One model that
has particular power over behavior is the Depression experience.

How many people do we know from the Depression generation who still hoard food and save string? Another common mental model of poverty is the immigrant story: people who have come to the United States in poverty and, in two or three generations, moved into a middle-class existence. Another model is the indentured servant who had to work for seven years to earn freedom. Slavery, followed by the Jim Crow days and institutional racism, is yet another model.

All of these mental models are valid, but none of them tells the story of what it's like to live in poverty today. This paper explores a new mental model of poverty that will enable us to study the impact of poverty on families.

MENTAL MODEL OF POVERTY

To learn about the impact of poverty on families, one can go to social science research, to those who comment on the research, and to those who have worked with families in poverty—all valuable sources of knowledge. In addition, one can go to those who know the most about it: families actually living in poverty now.

Throughout this paper, abstract knowledge is promoted and honored. The argument is made that a person must be able to use abstract representational systems in order to succeed in school, achieve at work, and make the transition out of poverty. Yet concrete knowledge is also valuable, especially when abstract information in the form of statistics removes learners so far from the actual experience that it loses all meaning. For example, data from the American Housing Survey reveal that 73 percent of people in poverty own cars or trucks, and 30 percent own two or more cars or trucks. This might suggest that poverty isn't all that bad after all (Rector 2004, p. 3). People with concrete poverty knowledge explain that those cars and trucks are anything but dependable. They are the cause of missed appointments, lost jobs, bruised knuckles, a stressful series of crises. The second car or truck is often the parts car. A mental model of poverty created by people in poverty illustrates what life is like (DeVol 2004, pp. 7-18).

MENTAL MODEL OF POVERTY

Developed by P. DeVol, 2006

The pieces of the pie are described below. Each piece, or element, is followed by concrete knowledge provided by people in poverty, then by examples of abstract knowledge that corresponds to it. Both forms of knowledge are necessary.

ELEMENT	CONCRETE KNOWLEDGE	ABSTRACT KNOWLEDGE
Cars and transportation	Vehicles are not dependable and require constant repair; breakdowns result in lost jobs, missed appointments, and stress. Insufficient public transportation limits mobility.	Cars purchased "as is" from buy-here, pay-here dealers come with interest rates as high as 15.5 percent (Shipler 2004, p. 27).
Housing	Houses are often in isolated rural areas or unsafe urban and suburban neighborhoods. Houses are crowded, people come and go, there is no private place for children to do their homework, rooms are used for many purposes, people sleep on the couch, repairs can't be made, landlord can be difficult, people have to move frequently.	Fifty-nine percent of people in poverty pay more than 50 percent of their income for housing (Dreier 2000). Affordable rental units have been on the decline since 1970 (Mattera 1990, pp. 128-129).

ELEMENT	CONCRETE KNOWLEDGE	ABSTRACT KNOWLEDGE
Jobs and money	Jobs don't pay enough, temp work doesn't provide enough hours or benefits, many work two jobs to make ends meet, no vacation. Money is a constant worry. People are vulnerable to the price of gas going to $2 (or more) a gallon and milk going to $3 a gallon.	Proportion of unemployed workers looking for a job for twenty-seven weeks or more: 23 percent, highest proportion in twenty years (Murphy 2004, p. 111).
		If the minimum wage ($5.15) kept pace with inflation, it would be more than $7.50 an hour or $15,000 a year (Bhargava 2004, p. A6).
		"… [M]ost available jobs had three unhappy traits: They paid low wages, offered no benefits, and led nowhere" (Shipler 2004, p. 40).
Food	There are concerns about not having enough. Grocery stores have moved out of the neighborhood. Local grocery stores that stayed overcharge, and the quality of produce is poor. Many must buy from convenience stores. Fast-food outlets provide relatively cheap but fattening food.	"Twenty-three percent of the nation's lower-income classes are obese, compared with 16 percent of the middle and upper classes … Large supermarket chains (the best bet for affordable, fresh and healthy foods) abandoned less affluent city neighborhoods, focusing instead on the suburbs … A 1997 USDA study found that food prices, including those for produce, are, on average, 10 percent higher in inner-city food markets than they are in the suburbs … There are three times as many supermarkets in wealthy neighbor-hoods as in poor ones, according to a 2002 study in the American Journal of Preventive Medicine …" (Goodman 2003, pp. 137-158).
Illness and health care	Being sick, caring for others who are sick, and trying to get healthcare are time-consuming and exhausting.	Poverty is associated with increased risks of cardiovascular disease, respiratory disease, ulcers, rheumatoid disorders, psychiatric diseases, and a number of types of cancer (Sapolsky 1998, p. 301).

ELEMENT	CONCRETE KNOWLEDGE	ABSTRACT KNOWLEDGE
Children	It's hard to get kids through the day; people have concerns about school, health, clothing, and safety. Childcare arrangements are unreliable, while good childcare either is unavailable or too expensive.	There are many more poor children in the United States than in most Western European countries. In the United States, one-fifth of all children live below the poverty level ..." (Lareau 2003, p. 28). "... [T]wo in every five children live in poor or near-poor families" (Duncan 1997, p. 3).
Safety, crime	Protecting your people and yourself is a constant concern. The criminal justice system is part of life; members of the family are in jail, on parole, or on probation. The drug culture is threatening.	Prison population: one in 143 adults in prison, an all-time high (Murphy 2004, p. 111). Sixty to seventy percent of people in prison are from poverty.
Friends and neighbors	Relationships are important. They are a resource needed for survival.	"... [I]nner-city social networks are not nearly as dense or effective as those Stack found in the late 1960s, for like the sprawling suburbs and small villages in the heartland, inner cities too have less social capital nowadays then they once did" (Putnam 2000, p. 317). "... [I]ndividuals who grow up in socially isolated rural and inner-city areas are held back, not merely because they tend to be financially and educationally deprived, but also because they are relatively poor in social ties that can provide a 'hand up'" (Putnam 2000, p. 319).
Entertainment	Entertainment takes many forms, including cable television, video games, drugs, alcohol, music, and spending time with friends.	Entertainment is a driving force for people in poverty. It helps them survive a very stressful life (Payne 2001).

ELEMENT	CONCRETE KNOWLEDGE	ABSTRACT KNOWLEDGE
Agency time	People in poverty typically go to three to nine agencies in the course of a year to get needs addressed. Each agency demands behavioral changes, a plan of action, and time for the activities listed in the plan.	"Much of human life consists of playing ... roles within specific institutions ... Individuals' chances of interacting with any given kind of institution are not random: Families from elite backgrounds tend to participate in institutions serving the elite, and families in poverty tend to be involved in institutions serving the poor ... [C]hildren grow up within a broad, highly stratified social system" (Lareau 2003, p. 15).

The following mental model is about the middle-class experience. Comparing and contrasting the mental models of poverty and middle class will help explain the different mindsets of the two populations.

MENTAL MODEL OF MIDDLE CLASS

Developed by P. DeVol, 2006

It goes without saying that there's a mental model for wealth too. Elements found in that mental model would include:

- Building and maintaining social, financial, and political connections.
- Meeting with financial and legal advisers.
- Managing homes and staff.
- Traveling internationally.
- Pursuing arts, leisure, and personal interests.

OBSERVATIONS

Elements that appear in all three models are family/friends, housing, safety, and children.

Elements found in middle class but not in poverty are education, housing as a form of building assets, jobs as careers, pursuit of interests and hobbies, insurance as a form of security, vacation and travel, and participation in clubs and civic organizations.

Elements found in poverty but not in middle class are agency time, car problems, concerns about food, health problems to the degree experienced in poverty, and the criminal justice system.

DISCUSSION

Interlocking: Elements of the model impact and influence other elements. Chain reactions are most severe in poverty where financial resources don't provide a cushion. For example, car problems or a breakdown in the childcare system will result in problems at work, which in turn may have a ripple effect across the whole system.

Vulnerability: For families in generational poverty, vulnerability is concrete and ever-present. For example, when the price of gasoline goes to $2 (or more) a gallon or milk goes to $3 a gallon, it hits people in poverty hard. For families in middle class, who can adjust to $2 a gallon for gas, vulnerability is an abstract concept, a future possibility to consider.

Relationships: Survival in poverty requires reliance on others. In middle class, the higher level of resources (such as insurance) allows one to be more self-sufficient. In poverty, people resources replace financial resources. It's not AAA that responds to calls for help when a car breaks down but a neighbor, family member, or friend. It's not the repair shop that fixes the car, but a friend with the know-how.

Change: Richard Farson, in *Management of the Absurd,* says, "The healthier you are psychologically, or the less you may seem to need to change, the more you can change" (Farson 1996, p. 85). It's one of the sad ironies of life that the more resources one has, the easier it is to change, while the fewer resources, the harder it is to change. This is a crucial concept because, in order for people to gain economic stability, they must change some of the things they're doing.

Tyranny of the moment: Peter Schwartz, a business writer, says, "The need to act overwhelms any willingness people have to learn" (Schwartz 1996, p. 231). This is the reason that education doesn't usually appear on the mental model for people in generational poverty. The daily pressure of survival in poverty requires that an individual be non-verbal and sensory-based. It keeps one focused on concrete problems, with no time for the abstract. On the other hand, survival at work and school requires that an individual be verbal and use abstract representational systems (Payne 2003).

No future, no choice, and no power: When attention must be focused on solving concrete, immediate problems, the view of the future becomes abstract. Families in generational poverty don't have clear future stories. Reacting to and solving concrete problems, which people in poverty are skilled at, is not the same thing as practicing choice, learning to be accountable for those choices, and developing the power to build a better future. Children in generational poverty grow up not witnessing or practicing that power.

Generational poverty and situational poverty are different. Generational poverty is defined as being in poverty for two generations or longer. Situational poverty is a shorter period of time and is caused by such circumstances as illness, divorce, debt, lost jobs, or death of a primary breadwinner.

SURVIVAL DEMANDS OF THE ENVIRONMENT CREATE THE HIDDEN RULES OF CLASS

The environment in which one is raised teaches the hidden rules of survival that are needed in that environment. In other words, economic realities described in the mental models developed earlier create the hidden rules. As stated at the outset, Ruby Payne defines and articulates these hidden rules of economic class. Hidden rules are the unspoken habits and cues of a group. They arise from cause-and-effect situations and reflect the mindsets that are needed to survive in that economic reality. There are hidden rules for race, nationality, region, age, sex, religion, and economic class. One need only be alive to learn them; they come to us by living, as if by osmosis.

All hidden rules influence behavior: One of the strongest influences is that of economic class. The hidden rules of class pervade the other rules to the extent that some middle-class African Americans have more in common with middle-class whites than they have in common with poor African Americans (Lareau 2003, p. 241). Churches divide and reassemble along economic-class lines; members aren't able to stay together beyond three of the nine economic classes. Paul Fussell defines the nine social classes as: Bottom and Out-of-Sight, Destitute, Low Proletarian, Proletarian, High Proletarian, Middle, Upper Middle, Upper Class, and Top Out-of-Sight (Fussell 1983). In this work we deal with only three economic classes: poverty, middle class, and wealth. Because hidden rules of economic class are so powerful in determining behavior, it's crucial that they be understood when a community decides to build sustainability.

NOTE: This work describes patterns of class behavior; there will always be exceptions.

FOOD

The hidden rule on food illustrates how environment shapes the rules. For families in poverty, there is no guarantee that there will always be enough to eat. Some weeks there is plenty to eat, while other weeks the food has to be stretched. Many children from poverty who live in middle-class foster homes are known to hoard food. In poverty, the focus is on the quantity of food. In middle class (where having food is a given), the focus is on the quality of the dish. In wealth (where quantity and quality are assured), the focus is on appearance and presentation.

FAMILY STRUCTURE

The different hidden rules for family functioning are just as understandable. In middle class, families tend to be patriarchal. The male gender role is that of provider; the female role is that of provider, homemaker, and nurturer. Children in an economically stable setting can expect their parents to support them financially, emotionally, and socially. Middle-class parents use a style of raising children termed "concerted cultivation" by Annette Lareau. These children are involved in 4.5 after-school activities a week under the supervision of adults: piano, dance, soccer, baseball, chess, church, Boy Scouts, Girl Scouts, 4-H, and so on. Parents and adult leaders engage children in discussions and analysis of performance at every opportunity. Parents in middle class are focused on the future well-being of their children (Lareau 2003).

Despite the pattern of marriage, divorce, remarriage, and the creation of blended families, most middle-class families are ever conscious of biological relationships and keep boundaries distinct between half-siblings and stepchildren. Middle-class parents will use the institutions of society throughout their lives; they go to religious and civil institutions to marry and the courts to get divorced. The biological focus is never lost because middle-class families have assets to pass on to their children.

All families have certain capabilities and strengths, and all families have to face such demands as accidents, illness, lost jobs, divorce, and death. When challenged by adversity, family members will adapt and take on new roles. As a result, families grow stronger. In effect, a balance is achieved between capabilities and demands. However, when there is an unrelenting cascade of demands, family resources and capabilities are swamped. Events that can bring this about are addiction, chronic mental or physical illness, and poverty (Henderson 1996, pp. 151-159).

Poverty itself is a stressor of such magnitude that it alone can change a family structure. When men do not have jobs with which they identify, the gender role shifts from provider to protector. Physical prowess, the ability to fight, and the role of lover are how a "real" man is defined. Men may take pride in doing hard and dangerous work, but they think of work as something that "I do for you."

In poverty, families tend to be matriarchal because men frequently are absent. Men are absent for many reasons. They may be looking for work, they may be in jail, or they may have to disappear for a time because someone is looking for them. Being a fighter/lover can mean that others have a reason to come after you. Men also may be absent because of policies that will deny resources to families if the man is present. The options for a man are to find another job, another town, or another woman.

The absence of men means that women are, by both choice and default, left to care for the children. Women in poverty become the keeper of the home, the keeper of the soul, the person of last resort, the rescuer, the problem solver. The matriarch's options when under stress are to get another man, get another job—and keep solving concrete, immediate problems.

Children in poverty are raised in the style termed "natural accomplishment." In this pattern, children are given love, shelter, and nourishment with the expectation that the children will grow up naturally. Children are in 1.2 after-school activities a week with adult supervision. Adult interactions with children are not focused on achievement and performance analysis but on casual interactions. Parents in poverty expect the schools to give their children the education they need and don't expect to play much of a role in the children's success in school (Lareau 2003).

The gender roles and other patterns that arise from this family structure do not prepare children very well to succeed in the larger society. The structure does, though, meet the survival needs—but only the survival needs—of the people in it.

DRIVING FORCES

In middle class, the driving forces are work and achievement. In poverty, the driving forces are survival, relationships, and entertainment. In wealth, the driving forces are social, financial, and political connections.

Survival, as a driving force for people in poverty, is easy to understand. Vulnerability in so many aspects of life requires immediate and concrete responses. Relationships provide resources and solutions that are often purchased by those with greater financial resources. But relationships do more than that; they provide identity, community, belonging, entertainment, and social standing. One needs others and, in turn, is needed by them.

When maintaining relationships becomes a driving force, it can interfere with achievement. Ruby Payne notes that, to achieve, people must give up relationships, at least for a period of time (Payne 2001). For example, to go to college means giving up time with high school friends and possibly one's parents. Leaving that circle for achievement of any sort (sobriety, education, work) carries some negative aspects, particularly the fear of losing others. This is difficult for people in poverty because of the importance of relationships; being there for others is as important as having those people there for you. When you stop spending time with your family and friends, the implication is that you have something "better" to do—that you would prefer to be with someone else.

Entertainment is a driving force (not just a pleasure deferred until work is done) because life in poverty tends to be unrelentingly stressful. While middle-class people can defer gratification with the certainty that the weekend will bring relief, poverty is a weeklong, month-long, and year-round experience. Jobs don't last long enough or pay enough to contemplate a two-week vacation that follows fifty weeks of work. Vacation must be taken every day—thus the indulgence in the least expensive forms of entertainment: TV with cable, games, drinking and drugs, bingo and the lottery, and the pursuit of sexual relationships.

MONEY

For those familiar with their own environment, but not the realities of poverty, the choices of people in poverty are baffling. The hidden rule for money in middle class is to manage it. So, when people in poverty spend what little disposable income they have on cigarettes, big-screen TVs, and cable, the middle-class rule is broken, and those who break it are criticized.

In poverty, the hidden rule for money is to spend it. Small amounts of money will not be enough to solve the deep financial problems of the family, so it should be used on the immediate needs of individuals in or near the family. Without the middle-class rules for money, even large windfalls will usually be spent quickly by people in poverty.

TIME

In middle class, people have enough resources and stability to take care of today so they can concern themselves with the future. In poverty, resources are so low that today must be the focus. People are busy stamping out fires. In wealth, the resources are so high that the present and the future are both secure and people can make their decisions according to family traditions.

According to Dutch-born U.S. artist Willem de Kooning, "The trouble with being poor is that it takes up all your time." Several problems arise from living in the tyranny of the moment, the first of which is that people in poverty break the first rule for work and school, which is never to be late.

Being focused on the present also makes it more difficult to plan; it's harder to calculate how long it takes to complete a task and to determine procedural steps with any certainty. Perhaps the most severe impact of poverty is that it robs people of their future story. As a result, people in poverty make decisions according to their feelings at the moment and their survival needs. This means that relationships and survival (the present) will trump time (the future) just about every time. For example, helping a neighbor get a car started is more important than being punctual for one's own appointment.

Schools, businesses—virtually all organizations—run on middle-class rules and norms.

DESTINY

Another benefit of stable resources as found in the middle class is the ability to make choices and have control over the direction of one's life. Children in middle class get to observe their parents as they make choices, plan, and fulfill their dreams. They themselves begin practicing choice making from their earliest days when asked, "What do you want for breakfast?" "Which of these two outfits do you want to wear?" Choices are tied to consequences, and middle-class children learn accountability to others and themselves early on.

By the time they're ready to fly from the nest, they have proved that they're responsible.

Poverty, on the other hand, demands reactions to crisis, and options are limited. Sometimes it's a choice between two bad options. The concrete problems that people in poverty solve are about the present; they aren't about the future. As a result, people find that nothing they do makes a difference. An inability to make things better, to see progress, makes it very easy to slip into a sense of "fatedness."

In an environment where choices are forced upon a person by circumstances—and inaction itself is a choice—accountability is hard to accept and enforce. Choice and consequence, accountability and responsibility thrive in stable environments.

Some people in wealth, particularly those from old money, have a sense of *noblesse oblige.* They recognize that they're privileged and, because of that status, feel an obligation to give something back. Every community has benefited from this in the form of public buildings, parks, museums, and support of certain organizations. Underlying this is a commitment to the community and its well-being.

POWER

For people in poverty, power is about respect for the individual. Showing disrespect for a person is an affront that must be challenged. To survive in poverty a person must be able to fight or have someone who will fight for them. Backing down is seen as weakness. So on the one hand the individual in poverty is very powerful, but at the community level, people in power have little influence, control, or power. In fact, many people in poverty are so powerless they can't stop bad things from happening to them.

Power for the middle class is in the institutions it runs, the information it holds, and the positions it holds. Respect for the individual is separated from respect for the position, so someone who is respected as a supervisor may not be respected as a person.

Power for those in wealth is about setting the direction for institutions, the community, and the nation. Personal safety and maintaining the *status quo* are primary concerns.

Many people in poverty have quit and lost jobs because of this hidden rule. Direction and oversight from a supervisor may be read as disrespect, in which case self-respect dictates action—speaking out, lashing out, or walking out.

POSSESSIONS

For the middle class, possessions are things—houses, boats, golf clubs, motorcycles, furnishings, and so on. For the wealthy, possessions are one-of-a-kind objects, pedigreed animals, properties, and businesses. For people in poverty, possessions tend to be people. The terms "my woman," "my man," and "my child" are often meant literally. Possessiveness grows out of the value placed on relationships and the resources that people represent. The more possessions (people) you have the better you are able to survive. Children raised with the hidden rules of poverty may be encouraged to value belonging over belongings. Most families in poverty spend more time together than families in middle class (Lareau 2003).

LANGUAGE

The middle class uses the formal register of language (proper syntax, large vocabulary, proper pronunciation) at work and at school for achievement. Formal register is the language of negotiation and is necessary for knowledge-sector jobs. The middle class (those who run community organizations and agencies) has important messages to convey to its customers and clients. Those messages are typically offered in formal register and the "let's get down to business," linear, sequential discourse pattern. Formal register, as explicit as it is, usually turns into meaningless noise in the ears of people from poverty (Sapolsky 1998, p. 306).

In poverty, casual register is used for survival and to enhance relationships. A working vocabulary of four hundred to eight hundred high-frequency words, coupled with a reliance on non-verbal communication and the reading of the social context, makes for a very accurate register. For example, intentions are more accurately and quickly read from body language than from spoken words.

Like all hidden rules, this one can result in misunderstandings, criticism, and broken relationships. It takes but a few seconds to determine which language register a person is using; judgments can follow just as quickly. This is particularly important because change (and almost all agencies that serve people in poverty require change) is only possible when there is a relationship of mutual respect. Relationships are based on communication, and communication is based on the appropriate use of both formal and casual registers.

Language ability and the number of abstract words an individual has access to is directly related to the level of education, and education is directly related to economic class (Payne 2003). It's during the first three years of life that thinking structures are being built in the brain. Research shows that children raised in welfare homes get a language experience that doesn't prepare them very well for the abstract, cognitive demands of school. Welfare parents tend to talk less to their children, compared with adults from middle class. A study by Hart and Risley found that children raised in welfare homes hear ten million words from their parents, while children from professional homes hear thirty million words in the their first three years. Children in welfare homes are familiar with one-word directions accompanied with a pointing finger, "Bathroom." In middle-class homes, the parents are more likely to mediate, identify the stimulus ("your hands are dirty"), provide the meaning ("we're going to eat"), and suggest a strategy ("so go wash your hands"). The nature of the interactions is also very different. In welfare homes, parents will prohibit their children from exploring language or their world twice for every one time they encourage them. In professional homes, the ratio is five encouragements for every prohibition (Hart 1995).

Children from poverty, therefore, are typically two years behind their peers and not ready for school. Children need to learn abstract representational systems from their parents because education is about learning and using those systems.

DISCUSSION

This brief discussion of some of the hidden rules identified by Payne provides a lens through which to explore the issues of family stability and community sustainability.

The hidden rules explain why the best indicator of where someone will end up is the class in which he/she was raised. Understanding and using the appropriate hidden rules of middle class and wealth will assist people in transition by giving them access to more situations and communities.

Knowledge of the mindset and hidden rules of each class leads to an understanding of others and ourselves.

An understanding of the hidden rules gives people a way to identify and resolve problems at home with family member, co-workers and employees, customers and clients, and in the community itself.

People in middle class need to know the hidden rules in order to make the transition to greater stability themselves and to assist people in poverty. Access to new situations and people adds up to more influence and power. With power come choice and the ability to change.

We shouldn't criticize another person's hidden rules because they may well be needed for survival in that environment. We can, however, offer another set of rules, another option.

The hidden rules should be presented as a choice, not as a necessary change in identity. The wider the range of responses a person has the more he/she can control his/her situation. People in poverty need to know the hidden rules in order to gain that power.

RESOURCES

This paper began by discussing the impact of poverty on children and families. Mental models of lower-income and middle-class experiences were used to express that knowledge, and the hidden rules of economic class were described. These things hint at the quality of life, but they do not define it. Quality of life can be defined in many ways; Ruby Payne defines it by the degree to which one has ten resources (Payne 2003). These resources cover all aspects of life and set before families and communities the challenge, in the broadest terms, of building the good life. She defines poverty as the extent to which a person does without resources.

One purpose of families and communities is to build resources, and that is the purpose of this paper. Building resources is the way out of poverty; building resources is also the way to create sustainable communities.

RESOURCES

Financial	Having the money to purchase goods and services, save for emergencies, and to invest. Having an understanding of how money works—being fiscally literate.
Emotional	Being able to choose and control emotional responses, particularly to negative situations, without engaging in self-destructive behavior. This is the "state of mind" that determines the way we think, feel, and behave at any given moment. It's an internal resource and shows itself through stamina, perseverance, and choice. This is about inter-personal skills for teamwork, teaching others, leadership, negotiation, and working with people from many backgrounds.
Mental	Having the mental abilities and skills (reading, writing, computing) to deal with daily life. This includes how much education and training a person has in order to compete in the workplace for well-paying jobs.
Spiritual	Believing in divine purpose and guidance and/or having a rich culture that offers support and guidance.
Physical	Having physical health and mobility.
Support Systems	Having social networks of trustworthiness and reciprocity that in-clude people from outside one's immediate circle. This is an external resource. Communities with rich social capital will improve life for everyone, even those with low personal social capital.
Relationships, Role Models	Having frequent access to people who are appropriate, who are nurturing to children, and who do not engage in self-destructive behavior.
Integrity, Trust	Trust is linked to two issues: predictability and safety. Can I know with some certainty that this person will do what he/she says? Can I predict with some accuracy that it will occur every time? The second part of the question is safety: Will I be safe with this person? This is an internal asset.
Motivation, Persistence	Having the energy and drive to prepare for, plan, and complete projects, jobs, and personal changes. This is another internal asset.
Knowledge of Hidden Rules	Knowing the unspoken cues and habits of both middle class and wealth.

WHERE RESOURCES COME FROM

Some resources are internal, coming from within the person. Some are external, coming from or being present in the family, neighbor-hood, and community. Some are both.

No one builds resources entirely on his/her own. Even physical beauty and high intelligence are genetic gifts from our parents.

As individuals we determine if we will utilize, even enhance, our resources.

Some families are building resources, passing on high internal and external assets to the next generation.

Some families are losing resources through accidents, illness, bad choices, and other circumstances, thus passing lower resources to the next generation.

ASSESSING RESOURCES

Agencies assess the resources of their clients as soon as they walk through the door. Financial resources are often the first to be assessed so the agency knows how to set the fee.

Each organization has its own focus, assessing some resources and not others.

Doing a self-assessment and investigating one's own life constitute the most meaningful assessment.

Assessing resources that are low across the board can be painful.

BUILDING RESOURCES

It's easier to build resources when you know the hidden rules of all three classes.

There are four common ways that people move out of poverty: an insight, goal, and determination to change; a particular talent or skill; a relationship with someone who guides and supports; and the pain of living in poverty. All of these ways are about utilizing and building resources.

Individuals can choose to build their own resources (for example, daily exercises to stay in shape, attending classes in money management).

Agencies can help people build resources. For example, mental health agencies can help individuals build emotional resources.

Communities can help citizens build resources. For example, communities can attract businesses that pay good wages, and communities can provide social capital through organizations that are inclusive of diverse people.

DISCUSSION

The greater one's resources, the better the quality of life. It stands to reason that good health is preferable to illness, that financial stability is preferable to lack of basic needs, that having many friends and acquaintances is preferable to being alone and without friends.

Poverty is not just about money. For example, it is possible to have very little money and be very high in other resources (for example, spiritual, mental, and emotional).

Likewise, it's possible to have strong financial resources and be spiritually impoverished.

Resources are interlocking. For example, a serious injury will suddenly lower one's physical resources and could negatively impact a person's income (financial resources), the ability to think and remember (mental resources), and one's social life (social support) if the injury stops the person from joining others in activities once enjoyed.

The greater the resources, the easier it is to build other resources. If one has high emotional resources, it's easier to get and keep a job. Many people have the mental capability to do the job but can't get along with others, so they lose their jobs.

The job of building resources is the responsibility of everyone: the individual, the family, the employer, and the community.

The following bar chart represents the resources of an individual on a five-point scale. It illustrates where the strengths and weaknesses lie and suggests which resources need to be increased.

MENTAL MODEL OF RESOURCES

	Financial	Emotional	Mental	Spiritual	Physical	Support System	Relationships	Hidden Rules	Integrity	Motivation
5					■					
4					■					■
3			■		■					■
2	■	■	■	■	■		■	■	■	■
1	■	■	■	■	■	■	■	■	■	■

MENTAL MODEL OF COMMUNITIES AT RISK

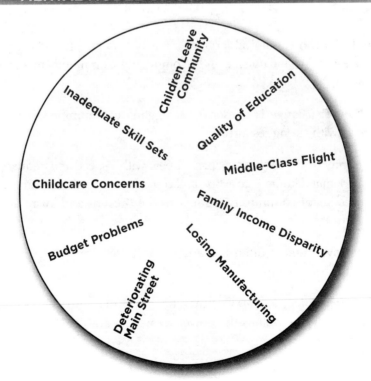

- Children Leave Community
- Inadequate Skill Sets
- Quality of Education
- Middle-Class Flight
- Childcare Concerns
- Family Income Disparity
- Budget Problems
- Losing Manufacturing
- Deteriorating Main Street

Just as we developed and learned from mental models of poverty, middle class, and wealth, we can learn from developing a mental model of communities at risk. Some communities are at more risk of becoming unsustainable than others. What do community members worry about? What is occurring that suggests problems?

DISCUSSION

Interlocking: Elements of the model impact and influence other elements. Middle-class flight to the suburbs in search of safe and good schools or jobs that have moved out of the city weakens the tax base and resources of the city. This breaks up neighborhoods that were once well-connected, as well as weakens the social capital.

Vulnerability: For communities that lose manufacturing firms, vulnerability is concrete. Some elements of the mental model are warning signs; some have the status of a red alert.

Relationships: Survival requires a reliance on people and organizations inside and outside of the community. Community members have a shared fate.

Change: Change is harder for struggling communities than for those with strong resources.

Tyranny of the moment: Crises appear with a speed and frequency that demand immediate action and concrete solutions, thus drawing the focus of community leaders to the present and away from the future.

Destiny: Choices often come down to a decision between two equally bad options.

Future, choice, power: Communities at risk may lose sight of their future story, as well as the power to make a positive future story come true.

EQUITY AND CRITICAL MASS

The interlocking nature of resources is a fact, not just for individuals and families in poverty but in whole communities as well. According to Thomas Sowell, if a community allows a group to be disenfranchised for any reason, the whole community becomes poorer (Sowell 1998). It works like this: When 10 percent of the community is in poverty, most people will say that there isn't any poverty. At 20 percent, most will still say that there isn't any poverty, but the social workers will be concerned. At 30 percent, people will say there's a little poverty, and the social workers will be extremely concerned. At 35-40 percent it hits critical mass and shows up on everyone's radar screen. The community takes notice. When poverty hits this point, the top 10 percent of the community will typically pass laws and ordinances to control the bottom 40 percent. These take the form of zero tolerance for drugs, no vagrancy, and no loitering. When 60 percent of the population is in poverty, the top 10 percent (which pays 70 percent of the federal taxes and has the most financial resources) will move away. In addition, many middle-class families move to the suburbs in search of better schools (Warren 2003, p. 8). That leaves the community with the population that has the fewest resources (the bottom 50 percent of households pay 4 percent of federal taxes). At that point the community is no longer sustainable (Payne 2004).

RESEARCH ON THE CAUSES OF POVERTY

When a family or community decides to build resources it will need to know what strategies to use. Too narrow a set of strategies … and the problem will persist. To define the parameters of the task we must understand the causes of poverty. David Shipler, author of *The Working Poor,* says that in the United States we're confused about the causes of poverty. As a result, we're confused about what to do about it (Shipler 2004). Clarity about poverty's causes is important. The research can be organized into four clusters, as presented in the following table.

CAUSES OF POVERTY			
Behaviors of the Individual	**Human and Social Capital in the Community**	**Exploitation**	**Political/ Economic Structures**
Definition: research on the choices, behaviors, characteristics, and habits of people in poverty.	**Definition:** research on the resources available to individuals, communities, and businesses.	**Definition:** research on how people in poverty are exploited because they are in poverty.	**Definition:** research on economic, political, and social policies at the international, national, state, and local levels.
Sample topics: Dependence on welfare Morality Crime Single parenthood Breakup of families Intergenerational character traits Work ethic Commitment to achievement Spending habits Addiction, mental illness, domestic violence Planning skills Orientation to the future Language experience	**Sample topics:** Intellectual capital Social capital Availability of jobs Availability of well-paying jobs Racism and discrimination Availability and quality of education Adequate skill sets Childcare for working families Decline in neighborhoods Decline in social morality Urbanization Suburbanization of manufacturing Middle-class flight City and regional planning	**Sample topics:** Drug trade Racism and discrimination Payday lenders Sub-prime lenders Lease/purchase outlets Gambling Temp work Sweatshops Sex trade Internet scams	**Sample topics:** Globalization Equity and growth Corporate influence on legislators Declining middle class De-industrialization Job loss Decline of unions Taxation patterns Salary ratio of CEO to line worker Immigration patterns Economic disparity Racism and discrimination

DISCOURSE ON THE CAUSES OF POVERTY

People representing the two ends of the continuum argue the causes and cures of poverty most ardently. One group argues that globalization and free-market strategies as they are being practiced today result in the loss of well-paying jobs—and that political/economic policies should be used to overcome poverty. The other group argues that poverty has to do with the choices of the poor. If they would just be punctual, sober, dependable, self-sufficient, and motivated, poverty would be reduced if not eliminated. Unfortunately, the two sides are making *either/or* assertions as if to say, *It's either this or that; this is true and that is not.*

Rather than being an either/or proposition, the research on poverty shows that it is a *both/and* reality. Poverty is about *both* the choices of the poor *and* the political/economic structures; and, furthermore, it is about everything in between. Poverty is caused by the choices of the poor, the lack of human and social capital, exploitation of the poor, and political/economic structures. There is good research in all four areas and therefore our communities must address all four areas when developing sustainable communities.

Alice O'Connor, author of *Poverty Knowledge,* says that our society has typically looked at poverty through the prism of race and gender. She suggests that another analytic category is needed, that of economic class (O'Connor 2001). Ruby Payne offers that prism; it is what informs this work.

Typically, communities put a great deal of effort into the first area of research: the behaviors of the individuals. Work-first was one of the key themes of the welfare reform act of 1996. TANF (Temporary Assistance to Needy Families) organizations focused on getting people to work. The idea was that getting a job, any job, and learning to work was more important than going to job training classes or receiving treatment. Community agencies offered treatment for substance abuse and mental health problems, money management classes, and programs to address literacy, teen pregnancies, language experience and more. The mission of these agencies is not to work directly on poverty issues, but to deal with co-existing problems. All of these agencies encourage their clients to change certain behaviors, recording and managing the changes through the use of plans and contracts. Many of the agencies hold their clients accountable for their choices and sanction clients who do not adhere to treatment plans.

Community efforts to enhance human and social capital include the strategies found in Head Start, WIA (Workforce Investment Act) programs, One-Stop centers, Earned Income Tax Credit and other anti-poverty programs. In this area too, accountability and sanctions are used to measure and motivate community organizations. Schools that meet certain benchmarks are taken over by state departments, TANF organizations that don't meet certain benchmarks don't receive incentive funds.

Communities rarely develop strategies to restrict, replace, or sanction those who exploit people in poverty. Even those organizations charged with fighting poverty sometimes neglect this cause of poverty. In part, this comes from departmentalizing our community services. People who work in organizations charged with serving those in poverty don't think of exploiters as their responsibility. That falls to law enforcement and policy makers.

Departmentalizing is even more pronounced when it comes to the causes of poverty that arise from political and economic structures. Community economic development is left to the market system, developers, businesses, corporations, the Chamber of Commerce, and elected officials. People who typically work with those in poverty don't see a role for themselves in the debate on economic development issues any more than those who are engaged in business ventures make a direct connection between their work and the well-being of people in poverty. And yet, in concrete terms, there is direct connection between the quality of life and the actions of government and business. For the person in poverty it comes down to this: A person can get vocational training in a particular skill, get a job, and still be in poverty.

This all-too-common reality is the reason why communities must develop strategies across all four areas of research, not just the first two. To continue to focus exclusively on the first two areas of research is to invite more of the same, more poverty. There is good research in all four areas; communities must develop strategies in all four areas if they are going to build resources and sustainability.

BARRIERS GENERATED BY POVERTY

We have already said that those who most need to change find it hardest to change. Making changes is very difficult for those in generational poverty. The following table lists the barriers to change that helping agencies will need to address to improve outcomes with people in poverty.

BARRIERS TO CHANGE			
Barriers Generated by Individuals in Poverty	Barriers Generated by Family and Social Network	Barriers Generated by Community Providers	Barriers Generated by Society
Crisis/survival/ reactive mode lifestyle	Resistance and sabotage by family and friends	Program theory based on middle-class mindsets	Departmental thinking and planning
Living in the moment	Penance/forgiveness discipline patterns	Clients perceived as "needy" recipients	Distrust of people in poverty
Low resources	Low social capital	Middle-class "noise"	Acceptance of those who exploit the weakest members of society
Polarized thinking	The need to earn respect of one's peers	Talents, skills, and abilities unrecognized	
Fatedness			
Not knowing how to plan	Not knowing the hidden rules of economic class	Organizational change difficult	Acceptance of high levels of poverty
Cognitive problems			
Co-existing problems		Departmental thinking and planning	
Not knowing the hidden rules of other classes			
Fear of losing others			
Fear of giving up identity			
Distrust of institutions			

DISCUSSION

- Many of the barriers listed above have not been explained in this paper.

- Front-line staff trained in poverty issues can address some of the barriers.

- Most barriers are program-design issues.

STRATEGIC BENCHMARKS

Strategies to build community sustainability can be organized to match up with the four clusters of research presented earlier. As noted, there is good research in each of the four areas, so communities must have strategies across the continuum of causes. Below are general benchmarks that point toward the action that will need to be taken. The specific programs and action steps will need to be decided by the community.

RESEARCH CATEGORY:
BEHAVIORS OF THE INDIVIDUAL AND FAMILY

- **People in poverty will have the opportunity to explore information that applies to their environment, family life, and community—and make plans for enhancing their own resources.**

  Rationale: People are more likely to develop and follow through on plans that come from a self-assessment of resources and their own analysis of the situation. Motivation is much more powerful when the individual makes the argument for change, not someone else (Miller 2002).

- **People will have the opportunity to learn the hidden rules of all economic classes.**

  Rationale: Knowledge of the hidden rules of different classes gives people a wider range of responses to any given situation. The wider the range of responses, the better one can navigate the world of school and work. Knowing the hidden rules makes it easier to build resources.

- **People in poverty will take the opportunity to build individual and family resources.**

  Rationale: In the end it's up to individuals to find the motivation and perseverance to make choices and take the action necessary to change the future.

- **Families will have the opportunity to learn how to enhance language experience for their children.**

  Rationale: One of the most direct and effective ways to help children have a positive experience at school—to win in that environment—is to give them a language experience that prepares them for learning. When parents are verbally responsive to their children, explain the world to them, and encourage them to talk they are preparing their children to succeed in school and in life.

- **People in poverty will have the opportunity to partner with the middle class and the affluent to build family resources and make a stronger community.**

  Rationale: One of the most immediate and successful ways to build resources is to develop bridging social capital with people outside of one's usual circle.

Enhancing Language Experience

In Morrow County, Ohio, low-income people are running three-day weekend retreats on how parents can be more responsive to children and how to enhance youngsters' language experience. Seven retreats have taken place to date, with more planned. The parents who run this program, once participants themselves, began taking over the roles of facilitating, organizing, and teaching at the second event. Now six parents and two agency staff run the programs and are paid well for their work.

The community agencies and schools continue to conduct the events using grant funds with the expectation that, in the years to come, everyone will benefit. Research done on the first two events shows that parents did become more responsive to their children. Children who are exposed to lots of talk, mediation, and formal story structures are prepared for school and will be well-received by their teachers (Hart 1995 and Lareau 2003). These children have the cognitive structures in place that allow them to store, retrieve, and manipulate information (Sharron 1996).

The program was designed by professionals who understood the hidden rules of economic class, along with the importance of resources, family structures, and language issues. In addition, the design was based on the knowledge that people in poverty are problem solvers.

RESEARCH CATEGORY: HUMAN AND SOCIAL CAPITAL

- Communities, businesses, government officials, and non-governmental organizations will establish mental models of poverty and prosperity.

  Rationale: Without a dialogue (total agreement is not necessary) on these core elements of community life, fragmented approaches will continue to produce disappointing results. The mental model of poverty describes what is; the mental model of prosperity defines the community's future story.

- **School- and community-based efforts to assist people in poverty will be coordinated.**

  Rationale: Many communities are already doing important things to address these issues. More coordination across departments could make them more effective. Coordinated efforts could include enhanced language experience for children, birth to age three; intervention strategies; development of public and bridging social capital; and the provision of ongoing, long-term support of people in transition.

- **Schools and communities will develop intellectual capital.**

  Rationale: Thomas Stewart, author of *Intellectual Capital: The New Wealth of Organizations*, defines intellectual capital as the "… intangible assets—the talents of its people, the efficacy of its management systems, the character of its relationships with its customers …" Ruby Payne notes that there is a direct correlation between the level of educational attainment in a community or country and its economic wealth (Payne 2004).

- **Programs will be based on shared principles.**

  Rationale: Communities need to be flexible in their approaches to economic sustainability. A rigid, over-planned, machinelike approach will work against community involvement and would be counter to the chaotic nature of community life.

  Guiding principles will help the process; programs will:

  - Be based on a mental model that recognizes people in poverty as problem solvers.
  - Teach the hidden rules of economic class to staff, customers, clients, and participants.

- □ Utilize the talents, skills, and gifts of participants.
- □ Assist people to establish a future story, practice choice, and plan.
- □ Bridge distrust.
- □ Communicate with mental models, not with an over-reliance on formal register.
- □ Provide opportunities for participants to earn respect with others as they make the transition.
- □ Build social capital.
- □ Assist low-income families to build assets.
- □ Provide long-term support for people in transition.

- **Businesses, chambers of commerce, and departments of development will adopt principles and practices that promote sustainability.**

  Rationale: The business sector, through its employment practices, contributes a foundational piece to quality of life through the quality of the jobs it offers, the wages it pays, and goals it seeks. Many businesses already subscribe to the worthy goals of financial returns, employee well-being, and community well-being.

- **Foundations encourage innovation in programming that will build community sustainability.**

  Rationale: Foundations provide direction and funding for community efforts and are often the catalyst for change. Free of government restrictions and departmental thinking, they can attract diverse groups to the table and address policy issues.

Retaining New Hires from Poverty

Cascade Engineering, a plastics firm in Grand Rapids, Michigan, raised its retention rate of new hires from poverty from 29 percent to 69 percent by applying Ruby Payne's concepts to the workplace. The welfare-to-career program includes these features: education on diversity and economic-class rules for all employees, long-term support for new hires through partnerships with community and government programs, mentoring efforts, accountability systems that support high performance standards that are designed to teach rather than discipline, and an accepting organizational culture (Bradley 2003).

RESEARCH CATEGORY: EXPLOITATION

- Legislators will protect people from exploitation.

  Rationale: Consistent, long-term protection requires legislation.

- Communities will replace what the predators provide with fair services.

  Rationale: Organizations that exploit people are delivering a service or product that is needed; an alternative is essential.

- Communities will not engage in the "race to the bottom" but will attract businesses that build community resources.

  Rationale: Selling local labor cheap contributes to the cycle of poverty and the breakdown of the community.

Fixing and Selling Cars at a Fair Price

Good News Garage in Burlington, Vermont, was started when the founder learned from a friend that she had purchased a car from a buy-here, pay-here car dealer that broke down two blocks from the dealer's lot. Good News Garage takes donated cars, fixes them, and sells them at a fair price with a warranty.

RESEARCH CATEGORY: POLITICAL/ECONOMIC STRUCTURES

- Legislators will pass legislation that supports the development of sustainable communities:

  Rationale: Those who set policy have the most influence over the well-being of communities and families. Principles for legislation should include:

  - Strategies across the entire research continuum on the causes of poverty.
  - Income support for low-wage workers.
  - Job training.
  - Childcare support for low-wage workers.
  - A measurement tool similar to the Social Health Index to monitor community well-being.

EVALUATION AND REPORTS

SOCIAL HEALTH INDEX

Communities need a way of measuring their success that is as broad as the strategies they undertake—and encompasses the wide spectrum of sustainability issues. The Social Health Index (SHI) fits that need. In the 1960s Minnesota Senator Walter Mondale and Wilbur Cohen, under secretary for the U.S. Department of Health, Education & Welfare, proposed the Social Health Index in the National Accounting Act. The U.S. Congress did not adopt the idea, but every other industrialized nation did (Miringoff 2000). The SHI covers:

QUALITY-OF-LIFE INDICATORS		
Infant mortality	Teenage birth	Violent crime
Child abuse	Unemployment	Alcohol-related traffic fatalities
Child poverty	Wages	Affordable housing
Youth suicide	Healthcare coverage	Inequality in family income
Teenage drug use	Age sixty-five-plus poverty	
High school dropouts	Life expectancy	

DISCUSSION

The SHI would provide data and reports in the same way that economic indicators are reported. There would be a Social Reserve, as there is a Federal Reserve; Leading Social Indicators, as there are Leading Economic Indicators; a Council of Social Advisers as there is a Council of Economic Advisers; and a Social Index similar to the Dow Jones Industrial average.

This would give communities, states, and the nation an ability to look at social issues in a more informed way: indicators instead of individual stories, conceptual stories instead of soap operas played out on the evening news, regular reports that show trends rather than episodic reports, and instant information rather than information that is months old.

The SHI would make it possible to get consistent reports, understand the evolving story, identify and respond to social recessions quickly, compare data between and among communities and states, deepen the discourse on sustainability issues, and enliven democracy.

Communities don't have to wait on a change in polices at the national level. More than eight hundred communities already have adopted the SHI or something similar to it. The information is available, but it's inside departmental silos at the local and state levels. Policies need to be adopted to institutionalize the SHI, and key economic indicators must be included in the data: unemployment, wages, healthcare coverage, affordable housing, and inequality in family income.

LIMITATIONS OF SOCIAL HEALTH INDEX

Like all other reports, plans, and evaluations the SHI is in danger of being put on the shelf and forgotten. The fact that it relies on hard data—information that can be provided by a few experts—almost ensures its shelf-bound fate. Reports, plans, and evaluations conducted by the few are used and remembered by the few. Other features of shelf bound documents are that they fulfill a management or accountability requirement, are done by outside experts, are based on past information, and present only quantitative information. To avoid the fate of other similar documents the SHI needs to be coupled with a process that enlivens it and makes it truly useful.

THE COMMUNITY-FOCUSED PROCESS

Albert Einstein said, "No problem can be solved from the same consciousness that created it."

The purpose of this paper has been to build a new consciousness of economic diversity and to present the interlocking nature of the problems faced by people in poverty and communities as a whole. This consciousness alone is not enough to successfully build sustainable communities. How the community approaches change is equally important as the knowledge itself. Old ways of problem solving are part of the old consciousness that created the poverty and problems that we have today. A new consciousness about how change can be achieved also is needed.

The process is as important as the product. One might say the process is the product. The process opens the door to other forms of knowledge: qualitative information, values, inventiveness, creativity, and new visions of the future. The goal is to engage the community as active participants in question making (rather than question asking), as sources of knowledge, as analysts, and as problem solvers. In essence, the process becomes part of the product and adds value to the SHI.

The idea of a community-focused process comes from the United Nations Development Programme, Office of Evaluation and Strategic Planning. It changes the roles of funders, evaluators, and community members as described in the following table.

PROCESS COMPARISON		
Roles	Top-Down Evaluation Process	Community-Focused Process
Funders: Government Foundations Local partnerships	Pay for the evaluation Set the evaluation guidelines	Provide financial support Act on recommendations Provide institutional support
Evaluators: Outside experts	Provide the report Participate on the evaluation team Provide credibility	Facilitate funder and community communication Facilitate evaluation process
Community: People from all economic groups	Provide information Question asker	Provide knowledge Question maker Conduct research Conduct analysis Provide recommendations

Adapted from Donnelly 1997

DISCUSSION

Community sustainability is so broad a topic that all components of society must be engaged in the process. This topic truly engages people from business, government, health care, criminal justice, education, and social services.

People living in survival mode will find it harder to become engaged in this work. The following will assist in getting people from poverty to participate:

- Direct-teach the hidden rules of economic class to all those involved in the process, including people from poverty. In this way everyone has a shared language and vocabulary to identify and resolve differences.

- Approach the poor as problem solvers, not victims.

- Start the process by building relationships of mutual respect, giving whatever time is necessary to know one another, using food and entertainment.

- Allow participants to bring their children.

- Identify and include the connectors (those people who know everyone), mavens (those who know what's going on in the community), and sales people (those who can sell ideas in the community) (Gladwell 2000).

- Utilize the talents, gifts, and skills of the individuals.

- Invite them to work on real (concrete) issues that impact day-to-day life.

- Have people from different backgrounds work on common tasks so that conversations take place and people get to know each another.

- When people become confident about what they have to offer at the concrete activities, encourage them to move to other committees and activities.

- Provide opportunities to earn the respect of peers.

- Teach question-making skills.

- Pay them for their time with inexpensive gift cards, gas vouchers, etc.

- Use mental models to help identify, with a minimum of emotion, the areas of needed change.

- Provide constructive outlets for frustration and criticism.

- Celebrate every step of the way.

PRINCIPLES OF CHANGE

Building sustainable communities is a matter of creating a critical mass of citizens who share the ideas about sustainability and are willing to change their behavior in ways that fit local circumstances (Taylor-Ide 2002). To guide the work, principles of change need to be identified, agreed upon, monitored, and revisited.

Principles of Change	Process of Change
Engage all economic classes in the effort. (People support what they create. Participation cannot be mandated from above or guided from the center; all levels must participate.)	Create a steering committee from a three-way partnership: people in the community, facilitators from the outside, and donors. Bring people in poverty into the process by sharing information about economic diversity with them, learning from them, and engaging them in concrete activities. All members of the three-way partnership must be "question makers." Question makers have a more active role in the process than "question askers" (Donnelly 1997). Identify what the sustainable community would look like in twenty years. Identify target SHI indicators and milestones.
Conduct whole-system planning to include all sectors: business, government, higher education, social services, schools, law enforcement, criminal justice, neighborhoods, faith-based community, civic groups, and others.	Whole-system planning utilizes charrettes, the decision-making strategy of architects, to involve everyone. For example, the plumber is not left out of the planning process when designing a building. Curitiba, Brazil (a city the size of Houston), began using whole-system planning in the '60s. SHI-style indicators for that city are very high. For example, Curitiba has the cleanest air in the world for any city its size (Hawkins 1999, pp. 285-308).
The process of change should be designed to cover twenty years so that the vision will extend into the next generation. (It takes time to build critical mass and resources.)	Use methods that are simple and involve many people. Create an ongoing cycle of evaluation, development, and improvement. Example: observation, hypothesis building, experimentation. Engage the entire community in the analysis phase.
Collect "real" community data.	Collect quantitative data for the SHI. Collect qualitative data from the community.

Principles of Change	Process of Change
Embed data, findings, and reports into community knowledge.	Open reports and records to the community.
	Make regular reports to the community.
	For example, reports on local SHI indicators would be used in local school math, science, and social studies curricula.
	Select a historian to chronicle the process, events, milestones, and outcomes.

DISCUSSION

A timeframe of twenty years moves the dialogue onto a higher plane, beyond the scope of quarterly numbers, terms of office, and typical accountability time frames.

Community sustainability is a concept above the fray of typical political discourse that defines a shared future.

ECONOMIC CLASS ROLES IN CREATING A SUSTAINABLE COMMUNITY

All economic groups will need to participate in the building of sustainable communities. The table below suggests the roles they might play.

Problem Solvers from Poverty	Problem Solvers from Middle Class	Problem Solvers from Wealth
Learn about economic diversity	Learn about economic diversity	Learn about economic diversity
Make plans to build personal resources Use personal and community resources to build personal and family resources	Make plans to build personal resources	Make plans to build personal resources
Assist agencies and organizations to design programs to better serve people in poverty	Train staff in economic diversity Design programs to better serve people in poverty	Assist agencies and organizations to design programs that help others build resource
Participate in community sustainability development activities	Influence policy development and legislation	Influence policy development and legislation to enhance well-being for people in poverty and for low-wage workers
Participate in problem solving	Encourage the development of community agencies and businesses that have worthy goals: the well-being of employees, clients, and community, as well as financial returns	Encourage the development of businesses that have worthy goals: financial returns, environmental performance, the well-being of employees, and the well-being of the community
Assist others in building resources	Assist others in building resources	Assist others in building resources

MENTAL MODEL OF
PERSONAL AND COMMUNITY RESPONSIBILITY
FOR A SUSTAINABLE COMMUNITY

The following model was created by a group of people in poverty who studied the information presented in this paper. The group developed a series of mental models to investigate the impact of poverty on themselves. They learned the hidden rules of class, did assessments of their own resources and the community, did an analysis of the information, developed detailed plans for the resources they thought they needed to enhance, and finally turned their attention to the needs of the community. Their mental model for prosperity is shared here as a proposal, a beginning point in the dialogue that must yet take place in each community. Like all mental models, it can be improved upon; other communities are invited to pick up their markers and get to work.

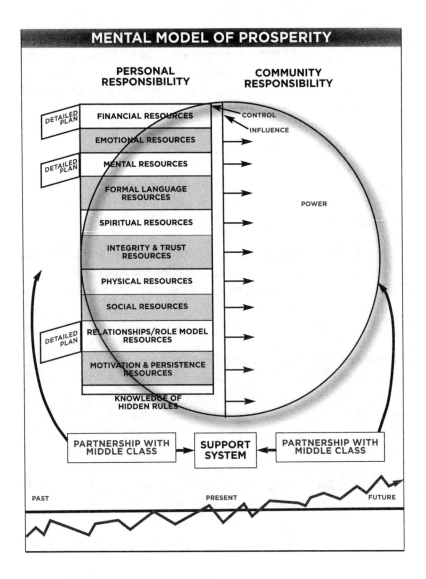

EXPLANATION OF THE MODEL

Personal responsibility: The left side of the oval is about the personal responsibility to build up low resources. All resources are shown to represent all quality-of-life issues; everyone's story is different. In the example three resources were selected for detailed development plans: financial, mental, and social resources.

Support system: The group members recognized that they needed long-term support for the development of the resources that cannot always be found in their own families. The support system they developed included internal, personal supports such as self-talk, backup plans, mentors, and the like. The external support system included people from their families and neighborhood who would support them, as well as others with whom they might develop bridging capital, such as mentors. Group members also recognized that they would need to partner with middle-class organizations and agencies that hold the information, power, and funding necessary to build their own resources.

Community responsibility: In recognition of the fact that poverty is about more than the choices of the poor, the group assigned half of the oval to the community. Again, members were interested and willing to partner with the middle class and wealthy to create well-paying jobs, affordable housing, and higher levels of social capital.

Influence and control: Group members recognized that those in poverty tend to have little influence or control over their lives. As their personal and community resources grow, they expect to see their influence and control grow too—thus the arrows pointing to the right, extending their resources and problem-solving power into new territory.

Time line: The trend line shows an upward trend in resources, with numerous ups and downs to reflect the reality of the transition process from poverty to prosperity. No one expects the process to be smooth or quick, and everyone expects to be in the process for a long time.

IN CONCLUSION

The first major revolution in the world was the agricultural revolution, the second was the industrial revolution, and the third is known as the information age. The next revolution is expected to be the development of sustainability.

It takes about one hundred years for an idea to reach critical mass. It took one hundred years from the abolition of slavery to the fulfillment of the civil-rights movement. It took one hundred years for women to win the right to vote. The idea of sustainable communities is in the same process. For some communities the issue is not even on the radar screen, while in others a desperate struggle for survival is taking place. In many more, the first signs of trouble are appearing. Communities that respond to the danger signs early will still have the resources and health to make changes; waiting too long could be fatal.

New strategies are called for, and all members of the community are needed to find a future story that will share prosperity and health with the next generation. It is encouraging to know that the future is not fixed. As Joseph Jaworski says in his book *Synchronicity,* "[O]ur mental model of the way the world works must shift from images of a clockwork, machinelike universe that is fixed and determined, to the model of a universe that is open, dynamic, interconnected, and full of living qualities ... Once we see this fundamentally open quality of the universe, it immediately opens us up to the potential for change; we see that the future is not fixed, and we shift from resignation to a sense of possibility. We are creating the future every moment" (Jaworski 1998).

WORKS CITED

Bhargava, D. (2004). How much is enough? *The American Prospect, 15*(9).

Bradley, J. R. (2003). Bridging the cultures of business and poverty: Welfare to career at Cascade Engineering, Inc. *Stanford Social Innovation Review.*

DeVol, P. E. (2004). *Facilitator notes for getting ahead in a just-gettin'-by world: Building your resources for a better life.* Highlands, TX: aha! Process.

Donnelly, J. (Ed.). (1997). *Who are the question-makers? A participatory evaluation handbook.* New York: Office of Evaluation and Strategic Planning, United Nations Development Program.

Dreier, P. (2000). Why America's workers can't pay the rent. *Dissent.*

Duncan, G. J., & Brooks-Gunn, J. (Eds.). (1997). *Consequences of growing up poor.* New York: Russell Sage Foundation.

Farson, R. (1997). *Management of the absurd: Paradoxes in leadership.* New York: Touchstone.

Fussell, P. (1983). *Class: A guide through the American status system.* New York: Touchstone.

Gladwell, M. (2000). *The tipping point: How little things make a big difference.* Boston: Little, Brown.

Goodman, L. (2003, December). A rotten deal. *Self.*

Hart, B., & Risley, T. R. (1995). *Meaningful differences in the everyday experience of young American children.* Baltimore: P. H. Brookes.

Hawkins, P., Lovins, A., & Lovins, L. H. (1999). *Natural capitalism: Creating the next Industrial Revolution.* Boston: Little, Brown.

Henderson, N. (1996). *Resiliency in schools: Making it happen for students and educators.* Thousand Oaks, CA: Corwin Press.

Jaworski, J. (1998). *Synchronicity: The inner path of leadership.* San Francisco: Berrett-Koehler.

Lareau, A. (2003). *Unequal childhoods: Class, race, and family life.* Berkeley, CA: University of California Press.

Lind, M. (2003). The new continental divide. *The Atlantic, 291*(1).

Lind, M. (2004). Are we still a middle-class nation? *The Atlantic, 293*(1).

Mattera, P. (1990). *Prosperity lost.* Reading, MA: Addison-Wesley.

Miller, W. R., & Rollnick, S. (2002). *Motivational interviewing: Preparing people for change* (2nd ed.). New York: Guilford Press.

Miringoff, M. (2000). *Census 2000 workshop.* Retrieved 2004, from http://www.jrn.columbia.edu/events/census/presenter/miringoff/index

Murphy, C. (2004). America's fortunes. *The Atlantic, 293*(1).

O'Connor, A. (2001). *Poverty knowledge: Social science, social policy, and the poor in twentieth-century U.S. history.* Princeton, N.J.: Princeton University Press.

Payne, R. K. (2003). *A framework for understanding poverty* (3rd rev. ed.). Highlands, TX: aha! Process.

Payne, R. K. (2004, October). Where do we go from here? How do communities develop intellectual capital and sustainability? *Bridges News.*

Payne, R. K., DeVol, P., & Smith, T. D. (2001). *Bridges out of poverty: Strategies for professionals and communities.* Highlands, TX: aha! Process.

Putnam, R. D. (2000). *Bowling alone: The collapse and revival of American community.* New York: Simon & Schuster.

Rector, R. E., & Johnson, K. A. (2004). *Understanding poverty in America.* Retrieved January 5, 2004, from http://www.heritage.org/Research/Welfare/bg1713.cfm

Sapolsky, R. M. (1998). *Why zebras don't get ulcers: An updated guide to stress, stress-related diseases, and coping.* New York: W. H. Freeman.

Schwartz, Peter. (1996). *The art of the long view: Planning for the future in an uncertain world.* New York: Currency-Doubleday.

Senge, P. M. (1990). *The fifth discipline: The art and practice of the learning organization.* New York: Doubleday.

Sharron, H., & Coulter, M. (1996). *Changing children's minds: Feuerstein's revolution in the teaching of intelligence.* Birmingham, England: Imaginative Minds.

Shipler, D. K. (2004). *The working poor: Invisible in America.* New York: Alfred A. Knopf.

Sowell, T. (1998, October 5). Race, culture, and equality. *Forbes.*

Taylor-Ide, D., & Taylor, C. E. (2002). *Just and lasting change: When communities own their futures.* Baltimore: Johns Hopkins University Press.

Warren, E., & Tyagi, A. W. (2003). *The two-income trap: Why middle class mothers and fathers are going broke.* New York: Basic Books.

■ ■ ■ ■

Organizing a Bridges community takes work, but the rewards are incredible. Boulder County has been so impressed with the Bridges constructs that the Community Services Department and Department of Health and Human Services have sent their staff to be trained. It has made a difference in the way we provide services in Boulder County.

–Janet Heimer, Director
Boulder County Community Action Programs
Boulder, Colorado

I have had the pleasure of facilitating the Bridges Out of Poverty concepts to over 500 investigators since 2006. These classes have been presented to a diverse population of front-line employees, students, teens, and upper management. As a result of attending the Getting Ahead classes, the participants have taken bold new steps in re-creating their lives by attaining more education and retraining for new careers. Outside of the changes that can be measured exist the many intangibles: the pride of achieving goals, inspiring peers, gaining social capital, and the power of self-discovery. This process is a journey that employs an investigative lens that has inspired many to move ahead toward sustainability as individuals and as a community. Bridges Out of Poverty provides a resourceful, investigative approach for identifying the causes of poverty, which is useful to inspire conversation around an inclusive round table of people working toward change.

–Lenore Moore, Bridges Out Of Poverty Trainer, Getting Ahead Facilitator
Youngstown, Ohio

Bridges has helped me discover a whole new sense of purpose. I now realize that being resourceful is a great strength. I am a single mom, a high school dropout, and a recovering addict. I decided to go back and get my GED, and I am now a full-time college student. I work for the Adult Education Enhancement Initiative Program. This job allows me to give back to the community and help people every day. I would like to be a social worker, and I can look forward to the future with an attitude of great possibility for myself, my family, and my community.

–Nichole Way, Getting Ahead Participant
Battle Creek, Michigan

I feel that this program really helped me a lot with knowledge I did not have before I took this class, especially in the area of life skills. So please, keep this program.

–Shaquin Caldwell, Syracuse Housing Authority, Getting Ahead Graduate
Syracuse, New York

2

GETTING AHEAD
PHILOSOPHY AND PROCESS

Excerpted from *Facilitator Notes for Getting Ahead in a Just-Gettin'-By World*, 2006

Thank you for taking on the important work of sharing the concepts of Dr. Ruby K. Payne with people in poverty. Being an early adopter—and adapter—of Ruby Payne's work is both a privilege and a challenge. It's a privilege to work on such an important issue, and it's a challenge because moving from poverty to prosperity is very hard to do. We will be working both with people in poverty and people in the community to make the transition possible.

This work can be a transforming experience for you, as well as the participants. If you choose to relax your professional boundaries a little you'll find that this will be a learning experience for you too. Also, the topics of poverty, prosperity, and community sustainability are so compelling that you will likely be challenged to expand your exploration of the topics and add to your reading list. This is not a scripted curriculum; it requires additional and deeper learning on the part of the facilitator.

THEORY OF CHANGE

If we agree on the theory of change that underlies this work it will allow us to be flexible and consistent in the way we present the information.

We will be sharing the theory of change with the participants, henceforth referred to as investigators, so they will understand what we are trying to do and so they can monitor their own progress as we move through the workbook.

Theories of change are often very involved and complex. In a way, ours is too, but it helps to state the case in as few words as possible, to boil it down to its essential ideas. Our theory starts with the way we understand the problem.

> *Poverty traps people in the tyranny of the moment, making it very difficult to attend to abstract information or plan for the future— the very things needed to build adequate resources and financial assets. There are many causes of poverty, some having to do with the choices of the poor, but most stemming from community conditions and political/economic structures. The theory of change must take all of this into account.*

OUR THEORY OF CHANGE

> *People in poverty need a safe space to analyze how poverty impacts individuals and communities and the opportunity to explore economic realities. This is a starting point both for reasoning and for developing plans for transition. Using mental models for comprehension and reasoning, people can move from the concrete to the abstract. Using Payne's definition of the resources necessary for a full life and her insights into the hidden rules of economic class, people can evaluate themselves, choose behaviors, and make plans to build resources and climb out of poverty. The community must provide services, support, and meaningful opportunities over the long term. In partnership with people from middle class and wealth, individuals in poverty can solve community **and** systemic problems that contribute to poverty.*

Getting Ahead in a Just-Gettin'-By World is designed to facilitate this theory of change. What follows is an expanded explanation of the theory. What appears in the *Getting Ahead* workbook is in **bold-face** type.

- Living in poverty makes it hard for people to change. The "What It's Like Now" experience is a trap that forces people to live in the moment and, in many cases, in chaos.

  Premise: The poor are trapped in the tyranny of survival, which demands concrete solutions and makes it difficult to attend to abstract concepts (Payne, Freire, Feuerstein, Galeano).

- Because of this, it is especially important that people in poverty explore the macro-economic issues of poverty, to learn that poverty is about more than the choices that individuals make.

  Premise: The research identifies many causes of poverty; therefore there must be a wide array of strategies to reduce poverty (O'Connor, Brouwer, Gans).

  Premise: The process of change is enhanced if the person can separate the problem from himself/herself (Freedman, Combs).

- It also is important to learn how poverty impacts individuals. So ... learning about the hidden rules of economic class, resources, family structure, and language issues is crucial to doing a critical analysis of the situation.

  Premise: Economic class is a unique analytic category for understanding and addressing poverty. Payne's work adds to the more typical categories of race, ethnicity, gender, age, and disability. The lens of economic class can be used to understand income and wealth disparity, the economic environments in which people live, and the hidden rules that arise from those environments. Knowledge of the hidden rules can make it possible for people from different classes to overcome their own judgmental attitudes and build relationships of mutual respect (Payne).

- **When people in poverty have the opportunity to analyze the macro issues of poverty, as well as the themes of their own lives, they will know what needs to be done.**

  Premise: People in poverty can be trusted to make good use of the information their Getting Ahead group produces in the co-investigative process with a facilitator who forms relationships of mutual respect (Johnson-Laird, Freire, Sapolsky, McKnight, Pransky, Farson).

  Premise: Individuals must generate their own motivation and plans for change (Miller).

  Premise: Mental models can be used to help people move from the concrete to the abstract to find new, yet concrete, solutions (Freire, Johnson-Laird, Harrison, Payne).

  Premise: Mental models help people learn quickly and without over-reliance on language (Payne, Freire, Feuerstein, Sapolsky, Mattaini).

- **Doing a self-assessment of personal resources and an assessment of community resources will allow individuals to make their own plans for economic stability.**

  Premise: Ultimately, the work of assessing and planning for all aspects of one's life lies with the individual (Freire, Andreas, Faulkner; Freedman, Combs; Miller, Rollnick).

- **Using the hidden rules of economic class to build resources will ease the transition to stability.**

  Premise: If people in poverty use Payne's definitions of hidden rules and resources, they will be able to more accurately assess their own internal and external assets and navigate middle-class systems more skillfully (Payne, Krabill).

- **Developing bridging social capital will enhance all educational, social, and employment endeavors.**

  Premise: No matter the economic class, people strive to earn the respect of their peers. A bridge of enhanced social capital is needed by which a person can earn respect in new places, with new people (Fussell, Putnam). Bridging capital makes it possible for people to come together across class lines to solve community problems.

Premise: Individuals who are in the process of developing their own economic security need support to stabilize situations during transitions (Payne). Bridging capital makes it possible for people to come together across class lines to solve community problems.

- **Working on individual plans is not enough because poverty is a systems problem too. Plans must be made to address community problems.**

  Premise: A partnership among all three economic classes is needed to bring about economic stability (Phillips).

  Premise: Mental models are necessary for the development of effective community strategies to build prosperity (Jaworski, Harrison, Senge).

- **People in poverty are problem solvers.**

  Premise: An accurate mental model of people in poverty is that they are community problem solvers as opposed to the prevailing perception that defines the poor as needy and deficient (McKnight, Pransky, Henderson).

PROCESS OF CHANGE

Sequence and reinforcement: *Getting Ahead* is presented in a particular sequence. It follows the pathway laid out by the first few groups to investigate poverty using this approach. It is important to follow the sequence and to reinforce the learning as you move along. Jane Vella, author of *Learning to Listen, Learning to Teach,* says, "When we work diligently to design learning tasks that are in simple and sound sequence and that reinforce learning, we address the disparity in political power more directly than if we preach loudly on social and economic injustice. These rather technical principles and practices—reinforcement and sequence—are tough to use. They demand attention and diligence to design. When you do that hard work, you are in fact addressing sociopolitical-economic inequalities. It is all of a piece."

The process: The triangle introduced in Module 1 describes how this theory of change is presented. In a nutshell it works like this:

- Learn about poverty in the broad sense.
- Learn Ruby Payne's framework.
- Learn how poverty impacts you.
- Assess your own resources.
- Assess community resources.
- Think about it; analyze it.
- Make your plans for building resources.
- Monitor your motivation and your changes throughout.

Trust the process: The first time you take a group through the workbook you are going to wonder if it's working. Questioning the process, along with feeling the urge to fix things, is natural. Resist the urge to react to all the things that worry you. After you've gone through the workbook a couple of times, you'll trust the process and let many things sort themselves out. Here are some thoughts to keep in mind:

This is a "kitchen table" learning experience for adults who are investigating new information in the context of their lives. It does not resemble in any way the typical classroom environment. There is no lecturing, no PowerPoint presentation, and no one standing at the head of the class.

People who go through this experience with you are to be referred to as investigators. Investigators are active; they question, they look into things, dig for facts, look for patterns, analyze the data, and find answers. These investigators will be examining their own lives and the conditions in their communities. Eventually they will be answerable to themselves, and it is anticipated that they will become problem solvers in their own community context.

This isn't group therapy, so it isn't your job to resolve longstanding emotional issues or even conflicts that people may have.

Some members of the group will have been in therapeutic groups, which can be helpful or unhelpful. On the positive side, they may have learned the responsibilities of group membership. On the negative side, they may need to be reminded of the nature and scope of this group and its rules.

Clarifying the group rules in the first session will go a long way toward preventing most problems. It's a good idea to review them from time to time.

Some members of the group will use the participatory discourse pattern and circular story pattern. When people arrive for the sessions (and sometimes even in the middle of the session) general talking or side conversations will likely break out. Most of these conversations have to do with survival; they're about a recent crisis, a relationship, or the sharing of survival tips. It's unlikely that any of these are about the abstract information contained in the workbook. It would be a mistake to treat this in a heavy-handed way when it's really an opportunity to learn. Don't miss the chance to learn something that might help you or the group—some nuance of predatory lending, for example, or an illustration of how a hidden rule was broken. Take a few minutes (no more than 5–8) for individuals to share with the larger group what you were overhearing. Write these things down on chart paper. Once these insights are listed, you can move on more quickly the next time the topic comes up. Anytime after the theory of change has been introduced, these conversations can be described as conversations about the "concrete." The more time spent talking about being stuck, the less time we have to talk about getting unstuck. *NOTE:* It also will be affirming to the individuals who share in this way that the "stuff" they bring naturally can and will be useful to the larger group.

Groups tend to act in predictable ways. The phases of most groups include:

Kissing up—Everyone tries hard to earn the respect of the leader and be helpful.

Storming—The rules are tested, and people assert their independence.

Norming—Patterns, rules, and unspoken rules are established and adhered to.

Performing—The members work hard, building on each other's ideas; people begin to appreciate each other.

All this can happen in a jury room, for example, as 12 strangers come together and start deliberating. Watch for these phases, keep notes on the process, and you'll likely see this unfold.

Participation in a group can be enhanced by the facilitator using the following kinds of strategies:

- Do a "round robin" at the beginning of each session, asking each person to answer a question. Some examples are … "What is one thing you remember from the last session? Is there anything going on with you that might make it difficult to pay attention today?" It's a good idea to establish a time limit on the answers! This gives everyone a chance to say something, to establish that he/she is "present" today.

- If someone is holding back, ask him/her what's up.

- Have people show "thumbs." Thumbs up, agree; thumbs down, disagree; thumbs to the side, neutral.

- Break the group into sets of two or three people and have them discuss a point and report back to the group.

- Ask for volunteers to assist you by writing on chart paper.

- When you start doing mental models, have people share theirs. The idea behind mental models is to use one another's thinking to build better models. Finally, don't forget that even the quiet group members are probably learning. If someone just doesn't want to verbalize, allow him/her to "pass."

Concrete to abstract to concrete: People in poverty live in the concrete but, if they're going to make changes, they need to be in the abstract where they can get new ideas. So … we offer the abstract in the form of research on the causes of poverty, Ruby Payne's framework, and information on how change takes place. Most people in poverty can't use the abstract unless it's made concrete and relevant. Because of this, we offer the concrete in the form of mental models, assessments, worksheets, and detailed planning steps.

Critical analysis: We trust that people can and will do an accurate analysis of the information and their situation—and that they'll know what needs to be done.

The stages of change: The stages introduced in Module 7 are: pre-contemplation, contemplation, preparation, action, and maintenance. This workbook is designed to take individuals up to and through the "preparation" stage. The "action" stage takes place when they leave the group, plan in hand. Maintenance, of course, comes even later. This workbook is about understanding, motivation, and empowerment. It gives people a vision and a taste of things to come.

Listening precedes dialogue, dialogue precedes action: We begin by listening, by reversing the flow of information. Listening bridges distrust and builds relationships. We don't leap to obvious conclusions or give people "the" solutions. People in poverty get enough of that from the agencies. Action—knowing what to do— arises out of the meaning of the dialogue.

Timeline: All of this is to occur in 15 sessions of 2½ hours each! The facilitator's greatest challenge is getting everything done in 15 sessions.

MOTIVATION

Our goal is for the investigators, not us, to make the argument for change. Our process is designed to promote motivation by creating a discrepancy between life as it is now and what it might be in the future. The "What It's Like Now" mental model created in Module 2 is the baseline for that discrepancy-making process. It names, describes, and analyzes the impact of poverty on the investigator. We must not allow ourselves to make the argument for change. Resist the urge!

The role of the facilitator is described best by William Miller and Stephen Rollnick in *Motivational Interviewing: Preparing People for Change.*

Carl Rogers articulated and tested a theory about critical counselor skills for facilitating change. He asserted that a client-centered interpersonal relationship—in which the counselor manifests three critical conditions—provides the ideal atmosphere for change to occur. Within the context of such a safe and supportive atmosphere, clients are free to explore their experiences openly and to reach resolutions of their own problems. The counselor's role, in Rogers' view, is not a directive one of providing solutions, suggestions, or analysis. Instead, the counselor need only offer these three critical conditions to prepare the way for natural change: accurate empathy, non-possessive warmth, and genuineness.

One of the unique features of our approach is that we pay people to participate in problem solving. This requires a rationale. But first, let's distinguish between motivation for change and an incentive to attend a workgroup. An incentive may get someone to attend a workgroup for 15 sessions; it is not sufficient to generate motivation to make life changes.

On the other hand, an individual is not likely to make life changes without getting new information that can only be obtained by attending.

RATIONALE FOR THE INCENTIVE OR PAYMENT

It's important to explain our reasoning for offering an incentive because a payment conflicts with the middle-class sensibility that says you shouldn't have to be paid to learn something that is going to better your life. Case in point: Middle-class students and their families pay for college, not the other way around.

People who live in poverty are living in the concrete, or what I call the "tyranny of the moment." The problems the investigators face require immediate action and, when a person must act, he/she will not be willing or able to learn. The security of a middle-class income allows people to know that today's needs are met so they can afford to focus on the future and the abstract.

Folks who live in the concrete can motivate themselves to move toward something or away from something. In either case, though, it's an immediate reaction. So asking people who are living in the unstable world of poverty to participate in a program that has some possible distant reward isn't going to work any more than the "thou shalts" of the middle class have worked.

This workbook is about change, and change is difficult for people in poverty. Richard Farson, author of *Management of the Absurd,* says that individuals with the most resources find it easiest to change; those with the least find it hardest. Incidentally, this is true of organizations too.

Paradoxically, for people to change (get sober, climb out of poverty, build assets) they have to move from the concrete to the abstract. So … helping people move into the abstract becomes a key issue.

People who run such programs have found that incentives are needed to get people to attend. Once a relationship is established, people may attend partly because of the relationship, because they like the instructor. When the value of the information is realized, however, that may become the greatest incentive.

Incentives are to be framed as payment for something that must be done, something beyond attendance. The investigator gets paid after each session, but that's only the "pay period." The work the investigators do is to create an assessment of the community and develop mental models for prosperity for themselves and the community. This sets up the expectation that investigators are to produce something and underscores the fact that they are problem solvers.

Finally, if the organization doesn't typically provide incentives for investigators, it may take a little creative thinking on the part of administrators and fiscal officers to get this done.

FACILITATOR ROLE AS SOMEONE
FROM DOMINANT CULTURE

Those who have worked on poverty or diversity issues are familiar with the quandary of the facilitator's hierarchical position. There is no escaping two conflicting and co-existing realities. One is the distrust that people in poverty have for authority and agencies. This can be ameliorated, but *only somewhat,* if the facilitator is from poverty, because he/she is an employee of an agency and/or he/she may be a member of some other group that disqualifies him/her from automatic credibility. The second reality is that people with more resources and a broader perspective have something of value to offer those who are trapped in the moment.

Freire's *Pedagogy of the Oppressed* contains the deepest exploration of this dilemma and the best guide for an educator or instructor. Dean Lobovits and John Prowell, writing about narrative approaches, offer guidance to the facilitator in their article "Unexpected Journey: Invitations to Diversity."

KEY CONCEPTS

Poverty in the United States is a complex, multi-layered problem that can be approached from many angles: race, ethnicity, gender, age, religion, sexual orientation, politics, and class. In Getting Ahead we use economic class as the analytic category while encouraging investigators and the facilitator to explore local cultural-diversity issues that arise.

Defining a dominated group: Members of a dominated group either share a common fate or are perceived by the dominant group to share a common fate. People from a distinct racial, ethnic, or religious group, such as recent immigrants from Cambodia or Africa, are likely to identify themselves with the group and recognize that their fates are linked. On the other hand, some people in poverty, even those of the same race or ethnic background, may not feel that their fates are linked. In other words, the individual *does* feel part of the dominant culture. Yet, it is the dominant culture that perceives him/her as a member of a group with a shared fate—as with poor whites, for example. When going through this workbook, some investigators may for the first time begin to identify themselves as being in poverty and as being part of a group with a shared fate. As facilitators, we need to be aware that this is occurring.

The implication for facilitators is this: If we don't acknowledge that some people feel dominated or threatened by us, and if we don't have a way of dealing with the dominator/dominated issue, we will fail to establish the relationship that enhances the transfer of information.

In addition, we as facilitators must be aware that if we aren't careful, we may contribute to the "false generosity" of the dominant culture. False generosity includes paternalistic attitudes and "caring for" strategies that are most easily spotted in the missionary to the "dark continent," but they're just as real in the mindset of many essentially good-hearted politicians and social workers here in the United States.

The fate of the middle class: As facilitators, it would be wise to consider the fate of the middle class. The middle class is declining for the first time since the beginning of the industrial revolution. Well-paying manufacturing jobs have gone overseas and now white-collar, knowledge-sector jobs, are going there too. The divide between the rich and poor occurs at the 10% mark. Ninety percent of us are sliding down as the top 10% are becoming increasingly wealthy. Several writers on economic issues suggest that the middle class should wake up; its fate is linked to that of the poor. The question becomes: Is this trend sustainable?

Education that transforms: In the foreword to *Pedagogy of the Oppressed*, Richard Shaull writes:

> *There is no such thing as a* neutral *educational process. Education either functions as an instrument that is used to facilitate the integrations of the younger generation into the logic of the present system and bring about conformity to it,* or *it becomes "the practice of freedom," the means by which men and women deal critically and creatively with reality and discover how to participate in the transformation of their world.*

One reason typical efforts to educate people in generational poverty have not worked is that they failed to challenge people to "deal critically and creatively with reality." Instead, they went straight to teaching the logic of the present system with classes in literacy, financial knowledge, job-seeking skills, workplace skills, and the like. This workbook is unique in that it deals with the realities of a political/economic system that contributes to poverty and trusts the investigators to analyze their situation, to solve problems, and to transform their world.

Two story lines: Facilitators will be working with two story lines throughout this workbook. One is the collective story of all people in poverty, starting with the creation of a mental model for poverty, then moving through the hidden rules of class and language experience. The second story line applies to individuals: their history, the impact that poverty has had on them, and the degree to which they do without specific resources.

In both these instances, the role of the facilitator will be to separate the problem from the person. In *Narrative Therapy: The Social Construction of Preferred Realities,* Jill Freedman and Gene Combs suggest that the way the questions are asked can facilitate change. When we ask, "How has poverty affected you?" we help create intellectual distance or detachment that *facilitates change.* This is different from laying the blame for a person's circumstances on him/her directly as if poverty had everything to do with the choices of the poor and nothing to do with larger community and national factors. Framing the questions in this way means that group members don't have to defend themselves.

Raising the difficult issues: As representatives of the dominant culture, facilitators need to be the ones to raise the issues that usually fall to the people in the dominated group: racism, predators, injustices, unfair banking practices, and so on. When those who are dominated raise these issues, it forces them into the role of complainer or radical—and may even suggest that they are speaking for the dominated group. Being forced into one of those roles takes away from any other role they might play: mediator, creative thinker, or leader. When the *facilitator* raises a controversial issue, the people from the dominated group are free to respond in any number of ways. In this workbook, the facilitator is the one who shares the details and historical trends of inadequate housing, low-wage jobs, and predators. The partnership between the facilitator and co-facilitator, who can act as a "bridging" person, can serve as an avenue for exploring the information and evaluating the relationship between the facilitator and the group.

Choice, power, and accountability: The main theme of our work is for investigators to analyze their own situations, assess their own resources, and choose their own plans of action. Facilitators will share the hidden rules of class and assist investigators to acquire the power they need to meet their goals. Power can take any number of forms, starting with power over oneself, as well as over one's own thinking and emotions. Then there is the power of language and negotiation and, finally, the power of connections and political/economic influence.

Linked to power and choice is responsibility … the responsibility for the outcomes and the actions that are taken. People who live reactive lives and have little opportunity to make significant choices—people who have little power or influence—are not likely to feel responsible for whatever occurs, for the outcomes. On the other hand, people who have practiced making choices and using power throughout their lives are more likely to be accountable to themselves and others.

"Accountability" is sweeping the land. Fourth-graders and their teachers are held accountable; people who seek work and their case-workers are held accountable; addicts and their counselors are held accountable. Accountability in its politicized form is greatly debated, clumsily done, and unevenly administered. For people in poverty, accountability is just another name for punishment; it's just one more time the middle class"lays down the law."

And yet, accountability is a positive attribute when it arises from within the person as a result of his/her use of choice and power. Facilitators need to hold to this form of accountability; it is a far better model than the"caring for"model, which fosters manipulation and dependency.

Our form of accountability has these characteristics:

- All information is presented in a way that is relevant, including information about accountability. For people in poverty, it has to apply to the concrete situation. This is one reason we hire co-facilitators from previous classes; they know how to make information more relevant.

- Expectations must be communicated clearly, concretely, and respectfully.

- Ideally, people will be accountable to themselves and others, perhaps even to the Getting Ahead group itself.

- The expectations are related to the systems and structures of the group, agency, community, or nation.

- People are met where they are. For example, for those who have mental health difficulties, addiction problems, or some sort of disability, the units of accountability are smaller and more immediate.

- Accountability is framed as choices with natural and logical consequences.

- Support must be provided for people who are learning to be accountable.

- When the above conditions are in place, people are held accountable for their choices. A consequence may be that they can't continue with the workgroup.

When any consequences are applied, they are handled face to face, not by letter. In this way mediation can occur, and the relationship can be maintained.

ROLE OF CO-FACILITATOR(S)

The first time you use the workbook you will be the only facilitator. The second and all subsequent times you will have one or two co-facilitators from the previous group or groups. It is part of our philosophy to use co-facilitators because they:

- Can make the material relevant.
- Can help bridge the initial distrust of the group members.
- Will learn the material more thoroughly by assisting as a co-facilitator.

- Will be building bridging social capital with you.
- Can earn respect by assisting you.
- Can help monitor and help improve the facilitator's performance as a member of the dominant class.

Co-facilitators will be paid to:

- Participate in the group just as anyone else does, doing the exercises, etc.

- Model how to explore ideas, how to be a healthy group member.

- Assist with getting ideas across in informal ways.

- Assist in evaluating and planning each session and, most importantly, will be required to ...

- Get together with investigators who miss a class to bring them up to speed with the rest of the group so that everyone arrives at the class ready to go—at the same place in the content of the workbook.

Depending on gifts, talents, skills, and interests of the co-facilitators, you may have them present information directly.

ROLE OF COMMUNITY AGENCIES AND ORGANIZATIONS

The groundwork done in the community prior to conducting a group will determine the experience and success of workgroup members during the action phase, which occurs after they have finished the workbook. Community agencies that share the aha! Process understanding of poverty, as well as the philosophy of this workbook, will be more likely to offer consistent approaches and support for workgroup members. Remember, the goal of this workbook is to help people develop specific goals for enhancing resources. Picture the investigators going to a community agency with their own plans in hand, motivated to utilize the resources offered by that agency. How that agency responds to someone motivated in that way can make a big difference to the person's future.

RECRUITING GROUP MEMBERS

As we begin using this workbook it's important to choose investigators, agencies, and communities carefully. That is to say, we'll want to start where we have a good chance of success, where the conditions favor the investigators. After gaining some experience with this new initiative, we can offer it to those who are in the worst trouble and who may need it the most. Here are some recruitment suggestions:

- Recruit from agencies that have a long-term relationship with clients, agencies that can provide sustained support as the investigators work through their plans. Housing programs, for example, often are engaged with people for as long as two years.

- Work with agencies with positive mental models of people in poverty, agencies that are most likely to share our philosophy.

- Work with organizations that are healthy and rich in resources. The healthier the organization and the more resources it has, the easier it will be for it to change its policies and procedures.

- If possible, recruit people who aren't experiencing a current mental health and/or substance abuse episode.

- Recruit people who want to participate. Using this workbook with coerced people is not recommended. If that becomes necessary, however, it would help if the facilitator were independent of the referring agency.

WHOM *NOT* TO WORK WITH OR RECRUIT FROM

- Do not recruit from agencies or communities that simply want people in poverty to "behave."

- Do not work with businesses, employers, and corporations that take advantage of employees by paying low wages, use temporary employees almost exclusively, and otherwise exploit people in poverty.

ACTION PHASE

When the investigators complete the workbook, the action phase of this process will begin. Putting the plan into action occurs when they leave the class. The transition from your group to the community is crucial to their success, and it's the facilitator's responsibility to prepare the way for the investigators with community agencies and organizations.

WHOM TO CONTACT

- Agencies that recruited investigators for your group.

- Agencies where investigators are most likely to go for help.

How to contact: Personal contacts are the best. People tend to pay attention to the things they give time to; ask for time to explain the project. Follow-up letters and phone calls will be necessary as the workgroup nears the end of the workbook.

WHAT TO COVER

- The process and goals for the workbook.

- The possibility that investigators may come to the agencies motivated to change according to their own plans.

- The possibility that investigators may be willing to "partner" with middle-class agencies and middle-class staff members.

- The possibility that investigators may use the hidden rules of class to resolve conflicts with middle-class organizations.

- The possibility that investigators may be able to build enough resources to end their reliance on the agencies.

- The possibility that investigators may be able to join the agency in solving community problems.

WHAT AGENCIES CAN DO TO ASSIST GETTING AHEAD INVESTIGATORS

- Build relationships of mutual respect and then ask about the plans made by the investigators.

- Accept their plans, i.e., work with whatever the investigators bring with them.

- Provide typical resources and services.

- Assign staff who can build relationships of mutual respect.

- Provide connections to new people who can support the investigators. Make room for investigators at the planning tables in the community. People who are typically at the table will need to "move over"—both physically and figuratively. The idea that people from poverty have something of value to share with the group is foreign to some people. It seems that we encounter our "isms" (classism, racism, sexism, and so on) when we're asked to listen to, learn from, and take direction from someone not of our "status." This "giving up of status" can be uncomfortable for people in the dominant culture. If it rankles, check it out. It could be a hidden "ism." As Getting Ahead facilitators, we can help facilitate understanding and transformation when we bring people from different classes together.

- Provide long-term persistence in support of the investigators' goals.

WORKBOOK LAYOUT

FIFTEEN SESSIONS!

Getting the workbook completed in 15 sessions will be a challenge. The content, duration, and intensity of the workbook should result in it making a lasting impression. Here are some suggestions for getting through the material:

- Meet with each potential investigator individually prior to the first session. Use that time to build a relationship, cover most of the content in Module 1, answer questions, and collect data and signatures.

- Schedule at least 2½ hours for the class so you can work for a full two hours. Take a short break during the session.

- As soon as the investigators grasp the material, move ahead—but encourage them to finish reading the text or do an exercise on their own.

- Assume people won't read much of the text; most of the learning will take place in the group sessions. Use the text as a guide.

- The first time you use the workbook you may need to schedule make-up sessions for people who miss a session to ensure you begin each session with everyone at the same place in the content. In later classes, you will be able to assign the catch-up session to your co-facilitators.

SUGGESTED SCHEDULE OF MODULES

Some modules will take longer to present than others. Here is a suggested schedule:

Session	Module
Signing Up/Orientation	Module 1, *portions of*
Session 1	Module 1, *continued* Module 2
Session 2	Module 2, *continued* Module 3
Session 3	Module 4
Session 4	Module 4, *continued*
Session 5	Module 5
Session 6	Module 5, *continued*
Session 7	Module 5, *continued* Module 6
Session 8	Module 6, *continued*
Session 9	Module 7
Session 10	Module 8
Session 11	Module 8, *continued* Module 9
Session 12	Module 9, *continued*
Session 13	Module 10 Module 11
Session 14	Module 11, *continued*
Session 15	Module 11, *continued* Module 12
Celebration	This can be part of the 15th session—or it can be a special gathering

PATTERNS IN THE WORKBOOK

Recognizing the patterns in the *Getting Ahead* workbook will help you and the investigators move through it more easily.

A few words about the title *Getting Ahead in a Just-Gettin'-By World: Building Your Resources for a Better Life* … The idea of "getting ahead" means action and movement—getting ahead of where you once were, not getting ahead of someone else. Survival living is when we are "just gettin' by" every day, which makes it the *world* of someone in poverty. It is also a *political/economic* world, which creates poverty and the just-gettin'-by conditions. The title hints at the discrepancy between what is and what could be. Moving from poverty to economic stability or prosperity doesn't require one to embrace "mad consumerism" or become middle class. It can be done by understanding the rules of money, living simply, and building the resources that Ruby Payne describes.

Language: The workbook was written in the formal register, with the expectation that the facilitator would translate the information into the casual register as needed. In other words, an investigator does not need to be literate in order to participate. Most of the learning will be done through the development of mental models that the investigators will help create. Investigators will learn the vocabulary and terms needed to be effective in community settings.

The triangle: Module 1 introduces the triangle that represents all the elements of the workbook. The triangle appears at the beginning of every module thereafter, except for modules 13–15, which are the closing, resources, and reading list. The triangle is to remind the reader which element we're working on: understanding poverty, understanding "where I am," critical thinking and power, responsibility, and planning.

Learning objectives: A "mediation" table appears at the beginning of each module. It follows the pattern of mediation that we have learned from Dr. Payne: the identification of the stimulus (the what), assigning meaning (the why), and providing a strategy (the how). In Getting Ahead, it takes the form of "what's covered" (a mini table of contents for the module), "why it's important" (the why), and "how it's connected to you" (how it can be used). Doing this mediation with the investigators will help organize the information and open a gateway in the brain for learning—the "why-I-should-learn-this" gate.

The content: The pattern for investigating information has the following elements and headings—information, discussion, activities, and reflections. The order of these is not absolutely consistent. For example, the information and discussion cycles may be repeated before conducting an activity.

- **Information:** This may take several forms, such as filling in the blanks, making lists, drawing mental models, or presentations by the facilitator.

- **Discussion:** The questions are designed to help people process the information. They are usually worded in such a way as to separate the problem from the person. It isn't necessary to ask and answer every question in the set.

- **Activities:** The most important activities are the mental models that investigators are asked to create. When the workbook is complete, each person should have a series of mental models that depict his/her life and plans. Some activities take the form of worksheets such as the worksheet on calculating the debt-to-income ratio.

- **Reflections:** At the end of each module, investigators are asked to think about how this information impacts them personally. It's OK to ask if anyone wants to share his/her insights with the group.

FACILITATOR SUPPORT

TIPS FOR RUNNING THE GROUP

- Establish rules that set boundaries and promote respect and safety.

- Establish patterns, rituals, and celebrations.

- Start each session with questions or activities that get everyone to speak so that everyone is established "from the gitgo" as a member of the group that day.

- Be tuned into the mood or underlying feeling in the room. Check with the group if the feeling is not "right."

- Start each session by getting agreement as to the agenda for the day and by discussing time frames.

- From time to time remind the group how many sessions are left. Start working on closure at the sixth or seventh session.

TROUBLESHOOTING

One of the best ways we can grow in our work is to share ideas and solve problems together. A community of practice is being created at the Getting Ahead website www.gettingaheadnetwork.com.

MODEL FIDELITY ELEMENTS
FOR CONDUCTING
GETTING AHEAD IN A JUST-GETTIN'-BY WORLD

Thanks to feedback from facilitators and sponsors who use Getting Ahead, we have learned what elements of our model are essential. In other words, we can now define our model. In order to adhere to our model, sponsors and facilitators are asked to attend to the following:

ROLE, RESPONSIBILITIES, AND SKILLS OF THE FACILITATOR

Problem solvers: Our view (or mental model) of Getting Ahead participants must be based on the understanding that they are problem solvers in their daily lives and can be problem solvers at the community level. They are needed at the planning tables in our communities.

Investigators: Getting Ahead participants are most accurately described as "investigators." They investigate community life, as well as their personal circumstances in light of the new learning they're doing. Each module is another layer of that investigation. It isn't the facilitator's job to defend everything in the workbook; it's the facilitator's job to help the investigators dig into the material.

Sequence and reinforcement: The sequence has been worked out carefully so that investigators move from the safe to the challenging, the concrete to the abstract, and the small to the large. It allows for reinforcement of the difficult concepts and is not to be altered.

Motivation for change: Those who participate in the workgroup are not expected to be motivated for change at the outset. The process and the facilitator assist people to make their own arguments for change. It isn't necessary for the facilitator to make the arguments; in fact, the facilitator is advised not to make the arguments for change. Facilitators who adhere to this model and have the ability to assist another person's process of self-discovery are to be prized.

Mental models: The investigators are asked to end the workgroup with mental models of their own making that describe their process, hold the knowledge of their investigation, and guide their action.

Self-assessment: Developing a plan without doing an accurate self-assessment is meaningless. The quality of the plan stems from the quality of thinking that goes into the assessment; therefore, it's necessary to practice analyzing resources using the case studies found in *Bridges Out of Poverty.*

Community assessment: This assessment is equally important and is to arise out of the work of the group. Community organizations should not be brought in for"dog and pony shows."

Personal and community plans: The ultimate goal is to create plans for building resources on personal and community levels.

Facilitator characteristics: Select facilitators who have the knowledge, skills, and attitudes described in "Getting Ahead Facilitator Qualities" (in Appendix J of *Facilitator Notes for Getting Ahead in a Just-Gettin'-By World*).

SPONSOR RESPONSIBILITIES

Attraction, not coercion: Planners are often pushed for quick results and think that forcing people to attend a particular workshop will bring the desired outcome. We, on the other hand, think this learning experience will attract people through word of mouth. Sanctions for failing to attend are unnecessary, even counterproductive.

Stipends: Administrators are often driven to be cost-effective. This means doing more with less—in this case, less money. Choosing not to pay stipends appears on the surface to be an easy solution. But paying stipends makes the point that people in poverty have something to offer the decision-making process in our communities, that the results of the Getting Ahead investigation have value, and that the investigators are being paid for their work.

Fifteen sessions: Another way of doing more for less is to reduce the amount of time given to the work, i.e., to cut down on the number of sessions. Fifteen weeks is the minimum amount of time needed to cover the information. We've learned that it works best to do Getting Ahead once or twice a week.

Closed group: There are two reasons for running the workbook with the same set of investigators from beginning to end. Having new people join the group means that they will not experience the sequence of learning as it works best. Second, the Getting Ahead process is based on a growing sense of trust and shared experiences.

Long-term support: The responsibility for this element falls on the sponsors of the workgroup more than on the facilitator. They are to be champions for the Getting Ahead investigators, making a place for them to build resources according to their own plans—and engaging the community to assist them during their transition. The investigators themselves may have plans of their own regarding long-term support; the sponsors are to be prepared to assist them.

Getting to the table: If the investigators want to take part in community planning and decision-making, i.e., if they want to "get to the table," the sponsor and facilitator need to be prepared to assist and mentor them, as well as to prepare the community for their participation.

BIBLIOGRAPHY

Alexie, Sherman. (1993). *The Lone Ranger and Tonto Fistfight in Heaven.* New York, NY: HarperPerennial.

Andreas, Steve, & Faulkner, Charles. (Eds.). (1994). *NLP: The New Technology of Achievement.* New York, NY: Quill.

Bonilla-Silva, Eduardo. (2003). *Racism Without Racists: Color-Blind Racism and the Persistence of Racial Inequality in the United States.* Lanham, MD: Rowman & Littlefield Publishers.

Brouwer, Steve. (1998). *Sharing the Pie: A Citizen's Guide to Wealth and Power in America.* New York, NY: Henry Holt & Company.

Covey, Stephen R. (1989). *The Seven Habits of Highly Effective People: Powerful Lessons in Personal Change.* New York, NY: Fireside Book, Simon & Schuster.

DeNavas-Walt, Carmen, Proctor, Bernadette D., & Lee, Cheryl Hill. (2005). *Income, Poverty, and Health Insurance Coverage in the United States: 2004.* Washington, DC: U.S. Census Bureau, Current Population Reports, pp. 60–229, U.S. Government Printing Office.

Farson, Richard. (1997). *Management of the Absurd: Paradoxes in Leadership.* New York, NY: Touchstone.

Freedman, Jill, & Combs, Gene. (1996). *Narrative Therapy: The Social Construction of Preferred Realities.* New York, NY: W.W. Norton & Company.

Freire, Paulo. (1999). *Pedagogy of the Oppressed.* New York, NY: The Continuum Publishing Company.

Fussell, Paul. (1983). *Class: A Guide Through the American Status System.* New York, NY: Touchstone.

Galeano, Eduardo. (1998). *Upside Down: A Primer for the Looking-Glass World.* New York, NY: Metropolitan Books.

Gans, Herbert J. (1995). *The War Against the Poor.* New York, NY: Basic Books.

Gladwell, Malcolm. (2005). The moral-hazard myth: the bad idea behind our failed health-care system. *The New Yorker.* August 29.

Gladwell, Malcolm. (2000). *The Tipping Point: How Little Things Can Make a Big Difference.* Boston, MA: Little, Brown & Company.

Glasmeier, Amy K. (2006). *An Atlas of Poverty in America: One Nation, Pulling Apart,* 1960–2003. New York, NY: Routledge Taylor & Francis Group.

Goleman, Daniel. (1995). *Emotional Intelligence.* New York, NY: Bantam Books.

Harrison, Lawrence E., & Huntington, Samuel P. (Eds.). (2000). *Culture Matters: How Values Shape Human Progress.* New York, NY: Basic Books.

Hart, Betty, & Risley, Todd R. (1995). *Meaningful Differences in the Everyday Experience of Young American Children.* Baltimore, MD: Paul H. Brookes Publishing Co.

Henderson, Nan (1996). *Resiliency in Schools: Making It Happen for Students and Educators.* Thousand Oaks, CA: Corwin Press.

Kahn, Si, & Minnich, Elizabeth. (2005). *The Fox in the Henhouse: How Privatization Threatens Democracy.* San Francisco, CA: Berrett-Koehler Publishers.

Kelly, Marjorie. (2001). *The Divine Right of Capital: Dethroning the Corporate Aristocracy.* San Francisco, CA: Berrett-Koehler Publishers.

Kretzmann, John, & McKnight, John. (1993). *Building Communities from the Inside Out: A Path Toward Finding and Mobilizing a Community's Assets.* Chicago, IL: ACTA Publications.

Kusserow, Adrie. (2005). The workings of class: how understanding a subtle difference between social classes can promote equality in the classroom— and beyond. *Stanford Social Innovation Review.* Stanford, CA: Stanford Graduate School of Business. www.ssireview.com (accessed Spring 2006).

Lareau, Annette. (2003). *Unequal Childhoods: Class, Race, and Family Life.* Berkeley, CA: University of California Press.

Lind, Michael. (2004). Are we still a middle-class nation? *The Atlantic.* Volume 293. Number 1. January-February. pp. 120–128.

Lobovits, Dean, & Prowell, John. *Unexpected Journey: Invitations to Diversity.* www.narrativeapproaches.com (accessed Spring 2006).

Lui, Meizhu, Robles, Barbara, Leondar-Wright, Betsy, Brewer, Rose, & Adamson, Rebecca. (2006). *The Color of Wealth: The Story Behind the U.S. Racial Wealth Divide.* New York, NY: The New Press.

Mattaini, Mark A. (1993). *More Than a Thousand Words: Graphics for Clinical Practice.* Washington, DC: NASW Press.

McCarthy, Bernice. (2000). *About Learning: 4MAT in the Classroom.* Chicago, IL: About Learning.

McKnight, John. (1995). *The Careless Society: Community and Its Counterfeits.* New York, NY: Basic Books.

Miller, William R., & Rollnick, Stephen. (2002). *Motivational Interviewing: Preparing People for Change,* Second Edition. New York, NY: Guilford Press.

Miringoff, Marc, & Miringoff, Marque-Luisa. (1999). *The Social Health of the Nation: How America Is Really Doing.* New York, NY: Oxford University Press.

O'Connor, Alice. (2001). *Poverty Knowledge: Social Science, Social Policy, and the Poor in Twentieth-Century U.S. History.* Princeton, NJ: Princeton University Press.

Phillips, Kevin. (2002). *Wealth and Democracy: A Political History of the American Rich.* New York, NY: Broadway Books.

Pransky, Jack. (1998). *Modello: A Story of Hope for the Inner-City and Beyond.* Cabot, VT: NEHRI Publications.

Putnam, Robert D. (2000). *Bowling Alone: the Collapse and Revival of American Community.* New York, NY: Simon & Schuster.

Sapolsky, Robert M. (1998). *Why Zebras Don't Get Ulcers: An Updated Guide to Stress, Stress-Related Diseases, and Coping.* New York, NY: W.H. Freeman & Company.

Senge, Peter M. (1994). *The Fifth Discipline: The Art & Practice of the Learning Organization.* New York, NY: Doubleday-Currency.

Sered, Susan Starr, & Fernandopulle, Rushika. (2005). *Uninsured in America: Life and Death in the Land of Opportunity.* Berkeley, CA: University of California Press.

Sharron, Howard, & Coulter, Martha. (1996). *Changing Children's Minds: Feuerstein's Revolution in the Teaching of Intelligence.* Birmingham, England: Imaginative Minds.

Shipler, David K. (2004). *The Working Poor: Invisible in America.* New York, NY: Alfred A. Knopf.

Vella, Jane. (2002). *Learning to Listen, Learning to Teach: The Power of Dialogue in Educating Adults.* San Francisco, CA: Jossey-Bass.

Wheatley, Margaret J. (1992). *Leadership and the New Science: Learning About Organization from an Orderly Universe.* San Francisco, CA: Berrett-Koehler Publishers.

World Bank. (2005). *World Development Report 2006: Equity and Development.* New York, NY: Oxford University Press.

■ ■ ■ ■

From the perspective of a well-seasoned social worker, the concepts of Bridges Out of Poverty provide people a wakeup call to societal patterns developed over decades. Those patterns include a separation from those different from ourselves, as well as our intellectualized rationales that allow us to maintain a judgmental distance. In the history of our social programs, we have given a "hand out" with the expectation that people will "come to their senses" and live according to our "right" way of thinking. With Bridges, the concept of "different but equal" lays a foundation for recognizing the potential in all people to offer solution—and to create a community in which we all can come together for the common good.

As a Bridges trainer, I have observed minds open to the possibility of change and watched people remove barriers to understanding those different from themselves. It has been a delight to see people living in poverty be recognized—and to recognize themselves as strong individuals with a voice—all of which will bear fruit in our common future.

–Jan Schaad, Licensed Clinical Social Worker
Cheyenne, Wyoming

For human service professionals who are often at the mercy of high caseloads, budget cuts, and professional burnout, Bridges offers real-world interventions with measurable results that can facilitate real change, not only for the client, but for the worker who rediscovers her passion for helping others. Bridges encourages a unified approach to community sustainability and provides the impetus for slamming the door on a "them and us" mentality … permanently. Instead, it gives us a broad opening for collaboration on all levels.

As a certified Bridges Out of Poverty trainer, I've had the distinct pleasure of introducing concepts from the book A Framework for Understanding Poverty to hundreds of Wyoming human service professionals, students, and community members. At each workshop, I celebrate the "aha!" moments that routinely occur when participants begin to challenge their own mental models about poverty, develop an appreciation for individuals who live in poverty, and embrace the power of human relationships.

I can't offer enough praise for the work of aha! Process. The work this organization does has the potential to positively impact millions of lives. I'm delighted to have been given the opportunity to be a part of it!

–Lisa M. Bunning, Project Coordinator
Wyoming Institute for Disabilities
Rock Springs, Wyoming

3

ADDITIVE MODEL:
AHA! PROCESS'S APPROACH TO
BUILDING SUSTAINABLE COMMUNITIES

Excerpted from *Bridges Out of Poverty*, 2006

The mission of aha! Process, Inc. is to positively impact
the education and lives of individuals in poverty around
the world. This mission is informed by the reality of life in
poverty, research on the causes of poverty, and Dr. Ruby K. Payne's
research and insights into economic diversity. The issues that
aha! Process addresses are economic stability; the development of
resources for individuals, families, and communities; and community
sustainability. aha! Process provides an additive model that recognizes people in poverty, middle class, and wealth as problem solvers.
The focus is on solutions, shared responsibilities, new insights, and
interdependence. This work is about connectedness and relationships; it is about "us."

USING THE KNOWLEDGE OF
PEOPLE IN POVERTY TO BUILD
AN ACCURATE MENTAL MODEL OF POVERTY

Going directly to people in generational poverty, the people working
the low-wage jobs, and listening to them talk about their concrete
experiences is to learn from the experts, the people with the knowledge. The circle of life for a family at the bottom of the economic
ladder is intense and stressful. Cars and public transportation are
unreliable and insufficient, low-wage jobs come and go, housing is
crowded and very costly, time and energy go into caring for the sick
and trying to get health care, and many of the interactions with the

dominant culture are demeaning and frustrating. For people in poverty, the arithmetic of life doesn't work. Housing costs are so high and wages so low that people have to double up, usually with family members, but often with people they may not know very well. All the elements in this mental model of poverty are interlocking: When the car won't start it sets off a chain reaction of missed appointments, being late to work, losing jobs, and searching for the next place to live. Vulnerability for people in poverty is concrete. When the price of gas goes to $2.50 a gallon it can mean having to work half a day to fill the tank. When one's attention is focused on the unfolding crisis of the day, people in poverty fall into what Paulo Freire calls the tyranny of the moment. Adds Peter Swartz: "The need to act overwhelms any willingness people have to learn." In this way poverty robs people of their future stories and the commitment to education. It requires them to use reactive skills, not true choice making, to survive. And finally, it robs them of power; the power to solve problems in such a way as to change the environment—or to make future stories come true.

By continuing to listen, one learns that people survive these circumstances by developing relationships of mutual reliance and facing down problems with courage and humor. It is family, friends, and acquaintances who give you a place to stay, food to eat, a ride to work, and help with your children. It's not Triple A that you call when your car breaks down; it's Uncle Ray. People in poverty are the masters at making relationships quickly. Above all, they are problem solvers; they solve immediate, concrete problems all day long.

Unfortunately, the current operating mental model of our society appears to be that people in poverty are needy, deficient, diseased, and not to be trusted. Again, this can be learned by simply listening: listening to policymakers, commentators, and taxpayers who don't want their tax dollars to go to someone who isn't trying, isn't motivated, is lazy, and so on. Another way to discover the underlying mental model is to observe its programs in action and work backwards. Three- to five-year lifetime limits for assistance, 90 days of services, work first …

These policies point to frustration felt by those whose mental model of the poor is that they are needy, deficient, and diseased.

This inaccurate mental model is fed by media reports that favor soap operas to conceptual stories and individual stories to trends and the broader influences. The public hears about a fictitious "welfare queen"but not comprehensive studies. What is needed is a thorough understanding of the research on poverty.

STUDYING POVERTY RESEARCH TO FURTHER INFORM THE WORK OF AHA! PROCESS

David Shipler, author of *The Working Poor*, says that in the United States we are confused about the causes of poverty and, as a result, are confused about what to do about poverty (Shipler, 2004). In the interest of a quick analysis of the research on poverty, we have organized the studies into the following four clusters:

- Behaviors of the individual
- Human and social capital in the community
- Exploitation
- Political/economic structures

For the last four decades discourse on poverty has been dominated by proponents of two areas of research: those who hold that the *true* cause of poverty is the behaviors of individuals and those who hold that the *true* cause of poverty is political/economic structures. The first argues that if people in poverty would simply be punctual, sober, and motivated, poverty would be reduced if not eliminated. For them, the answer is individual initiative. Voter opinion tends to mirror the research. Forty percent of voters say that poverty is largely due to the lack of effort on the part of the individual (Bostrom, 2005). At the other end of the continuum, the argument is that globalization, as it is currently practiced, results in the loss of manufacturing jobs, forcing communities to attract business by offering the labor of their people at the lowest wages, thus creating a situation where a person can work full time and still be in poverty. In a virtual dead heat with the countering theory, 39 percent of voters think that poverty is largely due to circumstances beyond the individual's control. Unfortunately, both two sides tend to make either/or assertions as if to say, *It's either this or that—as if "this" is true and "that" is not.*

Either/or assertions have not served us well; it must be recognized that causes of poverty are a both/and reality. Poverty is caused by both the behaviors of the individual and political/economic structures—and everything in between. Definitions for the four clusters of research and sample topics are provided in the table below.

CAUSES OF POVERTY			
Behaviors of the Individual	**Human and Social Capital in the Community**	**Exploitation**	**Political/ Economic Structures**
Definition: research on the choices, behaviors, characteristics, and habits of people in poverty.	**Definition:** research on the resources available to individuals, communities, and businesses.	**Definition:** research on how people in poverty are exploited because they are in poverty.	**Definition:** research on economic, political, and social policies at the international, national, state, and local levels.
Sample topics: Dependence on welfare Morality Crime Single parenthood Breakup of families Intergenerational character traits Work ethic Commitment to achievement Spending habits Addiction, mental illness, domestic violence Planning skills Orientation to the future Language experience	**Sample topics:** Intellectual capital Social capital Availability of jobs Availability of well-paying jobs Racism and discrimination Availability and quality of education Adequate skill sets Childcare for working families Decline in neighborhoods Decline in social morality Urbanization Suburbanization of manufacturing Middle-class flight City and regional planning	**Sample topics:** Drug trade Racism and discrimination Payday lenders Sub-prime lenders Lease/purchase outlets Gambling Temp work Sweatshops Sex trade Internet scams	**Sample topics:** Globalization Equity and growth Corporate influence on legislators Declining middle class De-industrialization Job loss Decline of unions Taxation patterns Salary ratio of CEO to line worker Immigration patterns Economic disparity Racism and discrimination

Typically, communities put a great deal of effort into the first area of research: the behaviors of the individuals. "Work first" was one of the key themes of the welfare reform act of 1996. TANF (Temporary Assistance to Needy Families) organizations focused on getting people to work. The idea was that getting a job, any job, and learning to work were more important than going to job-training classes or receiving treatment. Community agencies offered treatment for substance abuse and mental-health problems, money-management classes, and programs to address literacy, teen pregnancies, language experience, and more. The mission of these agencies is not to work directly on poverty issues but to deal with co-existing problems. All of these agencies encourage their clients to change behaviors, recording and managing the changes through the use of plans and contracts, and often sanction clients who fail to adhere to treatment plans.

Community efforts to enhance human and social capital include the strategies found in Head Start, WIA (Workforce Investment Act) programs, One-Stop centers, Earned Income Tax Credit, and other anti-poverty programs. In this area too, accountability and sanctions are used to measure and motivate community organizations. Schools that don't meet certain benchmarks are taken over by state departments; TANF organizations that don't meet certain benchmarks don't receive incentive funds. This isn't to make a blanket criticism of any of the programs that serve low-wage workers. In fact, many programs have great value to those who have used them. Rather, it's the almost exclusive focus on these two areas of research that is the problem.

Communities rarely develop strategies to restrict, replace, or sanction those who exploit people in poverty. Even those organizations charged with fighting poverty sometimes neglect this cause of poverty. In part, this comes from departmentalizing community services. People who work in organizations charged with serving those in poverty don't think of exploiters as their responsibility. That falls to law enforcement and policymakers.

Departmentalizing is even more pronounced when it comes to the causes of poverty that arise from political and economic structures. Community economic development is left to the market system, developers, businesses, corporations, the Chamber of Commerce, and elected officials. People who typically work with those in poverty don't see a role for themselves in the debate on economic development issues any more than those who are engaged in business ventures make a direct connection between their work and the well-being of people in poverty. And yet, in concrete terms, there is a direct connection between quality of life and the actions of government and business. For the person in poverty it comes down to this: A person can get vocational training in a particular skill, get a job, and still be in poverty.

This all-too-common reality is the reason why communities must develop strategies across all four areas of research, not just the first two. To continue to focus exclusively on the first two areas of research is to invite more of the same—in short, more poverty. There is good research in all four areas; communities must develop strategies in all four areas if they are going to build resources and sustainability.

Alice O'Connor, author of *Poverty Knowledge,* says our society has typically looked at poverty through the prism of race and gender. She suggests that another analytic category is needed, that of economic class (O'Connor, 2001). In her seminal 1996 work *A Framework for Understanding Poverty,* Ruby Payne offered that prism. Since then aha! Process has published many books and produced many videos and workbooks that are used to address poverty across all four areas of research.

THE NEED FOR CHANGE: NAMING PROBLEMS AND FINDING SOLUTIONS

Any community or organization that sets out to address poverty, education, health care, justice, or community sustainability must acknowledge that it seeks change: change in the individual's behavior, change in community approaches, and/or change in political/economic structures. Put another way, there is no agency that receives money—be it federal, state, or private—to keep behaviors and conditions exactly as they are. We seek change because we perceive something to be wrong.

Naming the problem is the first step toward a solution, and the most important step, for if the problem is not named accurately the course of action based on that faulty assumption will only lead further and further from a solution. So naming problems accurately—making the correct diagnosis—is crucial because it is on those definitions that the theories of change and program activities are based.

But naming the problem isn't as simple as it seems. If a problem exists, is it due to something that is lacking, a shortage, a disadvantage, a handicap? It is here that planners, providers, and problem solvers tend to slide into what often is referred to as the deficit model. This model seems to derive from what William Miller calls the righting reflex. He says, "Human beings seem to have a built-in desire to set things right" (Miller, 2002). We see something that is wrong; we want to fix it. This tendency is all well and good as long as it's confined to one's own problems, but as soon as our fix-it intentions are focused on others, this approach quickly loses its charm and questions arise. Who is it that names the problem? Who is it a problem for? What evidence is provided? How broad or deep is the investigation? People from minority cultures and dominated groups are the first to ask these questions, for it is often their ways of raising children, their language uses, and their problem-solving strategies that are being labeled as having deficits by the mainstream culture. Nobody likes deficit labeling. So it is that the righting reflex leads to deficit models that few of us like—and even fewer defend, for good reasons.

There is no known father or mother of the deficit model. Nobody claims it, but the title or slur gets hung around the neck of those who use it, or appear to use it. Some people hold that James Coleman, who has been called the "father of busing," proposed a deficit model. A review of the body of his work would refute that label. His research on education, one of the largest research projects ever undertaken, discussed economic class and achievement in its complexities. It was legislators, businesspeople, school administrators, and others who were under pressure to "Fix it!" who simplified Coleman's work when they turned it into policy. There are two things to be learned from this. First, the deficit model is simplistic; it oversimplifies the research and applies the righting reflex. Second, there is research—and then there are those who use the research.

It's important to take a closer look at how problems get named and what the distinction is between naming problems and deficit labeling. The deficit model names the problem and blames the individual; the individual must change, whereas society can be left unaltered. It is, however, possible to name problems and not blame the individual. For example, Dr. James P. Comer, not by any stretch a proponent of the deficit model, does identify the family environment as crucial to a child's academic success. He points to hard science—brain research—that confirms the interactive process between the mediation (interpretation of reality) that children receive from caregivers before they come to school with the continuous mediation when children enter school. Quoting Comer: "Without [mediation] children can lose the 'sense'—the intelligence potential—they were born with. Children who have had positive developmental experiences before starting school acquire a set of beliefs, attitudes, and values—as well as social, verbal, and problem-solving skills, connections, and power—that they can use to succeed in school. They are the ones best able to elicit a positive response from people at school and bond with them." Read another way, this could appear as labeling low-income families with deficits. Of course, it isn't that because Comer acknowledges the problems that exist across the system; it's never as simple as the fault of a single person or group. The body of Comer's work reveals the true nature of his model (Comer, 2001).

Despite the fact that the deficit model seems to have no father or mother and is the work of policymakers more than researchers (and gets confused with the naming of problems), the deficit model is still for real. Its features are that it fixes the problems on the individual and therefore focuses on fixing the individual. Environmental conditions are translated into the characteristics of the individual and gradually turn into negative stereotypes. The talents, gifts, and skills of an individual get lost. In the deficit model the "glass is seen as half empty." The message becomes "you can't," and the impulse to care for and protect arises. Thus we have "special needs," "special programs," "special rooms," and "special personnel," all of which can lead to and foster dependency.

The lack of staff training can result in the deficit model appearing in the attitudes of the professionals, in individual bias, and inaccurate assumptions. Notes Comer: "Many successful people are inclined to attribute their situations to their own ability and effort—making them, in their minds, more deserving than less successful people. They ignore the support they received from families, networks of friends and kin, schools, and powerful others. They see no need for improved support of youth development" (Comer, 2001). Without training, staff members are likely to see deficits where there are none. A child who comes to school after getting up early to pump water from an outside well and whose mother hand-washes clothes once a week may be seen as dirty, less presentable, more lacking in physical resources than children who can shower in their own bathroom before coming to school and whose mother uses a washer and dryer. The first child has the resources and skills but isn't readily able to demonstrate those capabilities.

The lack of understanding on the part of the staff can lead to labeling that is hard to shake. If the school or agency doesn't provide some way for individuals to demonstrate their skills and resources, the glass will always appear to be half empty.

Problems are identified with student performance, drug use, teen pregnancy, inadequate skill sets, job retention, criminal behavior, poverty, and so on, all of which gives rise to fix-it programs. One

Teacher Leaders Network online discussion participant offered this analogy about deficit-model programs: "We call it the 'chicken inspector' mindset. You see, the chicken inspector has been trained to look for something that isn't right, so that's his focus and that's what he finds—the things that are wrong. The more things he finds wrong, the better he feels he is doing his job."

The deficit model finds its way into the design of programs. Legislators and professionals set policy and create departments and programs. Each department is expected to fix the piece of the pie that falls under its purview. These reactions to the latest problem set up a random approach to problem solving and result in remedial programs focused on the behaviors of the individual while losing sight of the whole system made up of families, neighborhoods, communities, and sociopolitical/economic structures.

This isn't to suggest that policymakers and program designers set out to apply the deficit model. It's more likely that they select some other approach but for any number of reasons fail to adhere to their espoused theory (what is said) and slide into a "theory of use" (what is done) that resembles the deficit model (Senge, 1994). Perhaps the most common reason for this slip is that it's easier to describe, plan for, monitor, and sanction the behaviors of individuals than it is to hold organizations, communities, and systems accountable in the same way (Washburne, 1958). The fact is that the deficit model is resilient, and we slide back into it easily.

Opposite the deficit model are many models that offer what the deficit model does not. They go by many names: positive model, developmental assets, competency, value-based, and strength-based … to name a few. Other models have been assigned names by their developers: Health Realization, Resiliency in Action, Comer Model, and Motivational Interviewing to name but four. Each of these models has its distinct theory and practices, but the one thing they have in common is that they see "the glass as half full."

Positive models too are not without their critics. For example, child-protection workers point out that reframing the behaviors and characteristics of victims of abuse into strengths is naïve. No matter how resilient the child, the fact remains that the child has very little control over his/her environment and the behaviors of adults. Educators note that children in poverty have been exposed to more in their few years than many adults. In some ways they seem to have adult capabilities; they take care of themselves and feel confident they can handle big decisions. But the educators caution against accepting this claim. According to a recent piece by Craig Sautter, "We as adults need to remember that they are not adults. They still have a lot of growing and developing to do and still need the guidance of adults who can be there to help them through their growing-up period" (Sautter, 2005).

The additive model, a term used by Ruby Payne to describe the work of her company, aha! Process, combines the value of accurate problem identification with a positive, strength-based, communitywide approach to change.

To survive in poverty, individuals must have reactive, sensory, and non-verbal skills. This means people have the ability to read situations, establish relationships, and solve immediate and concrete problems quickly. People in the unstable, vulnerable, unpredictable world of poverty use reactive skills to fix problems on the fly. In that environment, individuals have a full glass; they have the assets, resiliency, and strengths to survive.

When individuals in poverty encounter the middle-class world of work, school, and all the other institutions of the land, he or she may not have all experience or knowledge to navigate the institutions confidently. The stable and predictable environment of the middle class requires and supports proactive, abstract, and verbal skills. The additive model offers insight into how hidden rules of economic class work, along with a framework for building resources, a way to fill up the glass.

When the person in middle class encounters wealth, the same is true—but to a greater extent.

Individuals raised in a middle-class environment learn the hidden rules, mindsets, and means of survival the same way persons in poverty or wealth do: through osmosis. To learn the survival rules of one's environment, virtually all one has to do is breathe. So the glass is full so long as individuals remain in their environment. But should middle class individuals suddenly find themselves in poverty—or even in a poverty neighborhood—would they have the assets needed to survive there? The glass would be half empty. But there is a more common scenario that brings people in middle class and people in poverty together; that is in the institutions run by middle-class people. In this scenario both groups come with a glass half full because they may not understand the rules or value the assets of the other person or the other class. Here is where the additive model can help. It names the problem and offers insight and awareness; it opens the way to build relationships and eventually to better outcomes for both.

As middle-class individuals interact with people in wealth they may not know any more about the rules of survival in wealth than the person in poverty knows about the rules of middle class (and how the values of the additive model apply).

The additive model has something to offer people in wealth as well. Where the worlds of wealth, middle class, and poverty intersect, the additive model can be helpful. Due to their connections, influence, and power, people in wealth are often in the position to design the policies and directions of the institutions that the middle class run and that the people in poverty use. If wealthy and middle class individuals do not have an accurate understanding of the impact of poverty on individuals and if they have normalized their stable environments to the extent that they assume that everyone (including people in poverty) experience society has they do the resulting policies and programs will be ineffective and even counterproductive.

To better understand the additive model, we must consider aha! Process definitions and core concepts.

RESOURCES

Resources: The following resources are quality-of-life indicators that are described in almost all aha! Process publications.

Financial	Physical
Emotional	Support systems
Mental	Relationships/role models
Spiritual	Knowledge of hidden rules

Poverty: the extent to which an individual or community does without these resources.

Prosperity/sustainability: the extent to which an individual or community has these resources.

By these definitions it is easy to see that an individual may have low financial resources and at the same time have other resources that are very high. Of course, the opposite is true too: One can have high financial resources and be impoverished in other ways.

This approach emphasizes that every individual's story is different and takes into account the environment in which one lives. And yet, as a general rule, the additive model holds that to have high resources is better than to not have high resources. It's preferable to have financial stability than to be unable to pay for basic needs. It's preferable to have many positive relationships than to live in isolation. It's preferable to be able to identify feelings, choose behaviors, and get along with others than to be emotionally destructive.

The additive model holds that:

- Resources are to be developed by communities, families, and individuals. In fact, it is the appropriate role, or "job" if you will, of individuals, families, and communities to grow resources for oneself, one's family, and the community.

- The optimal way to build resources is to build on one's strengths. Focusing on low resources, weaknesses, and what is absent not only is no fun, it simply isn't effective.

- We must develop resource-building strategies across all four areas of poverty research. The deficit model is at work when a community focuses its anti-poverty strategies on the behaviors of the individual.

Ruby Payne's research on the hidden rules of economic class is another key component of the aha! Process approach. It is this analytic category that provides a new lens through which to examine poverty and prosperity issues. Again, some definitions will help clarify the additive model.

HIDDEN RULES OF ECONOMIC CLASS

Hidden rules: the unspoken cues and habits of a group. All groups have hidden rules; you know you belong when you don't have to explain anything you say or do. These rules are held by racial, ethnic, religious, regional, and cultural groups … to name a few. An individual's cultural fabric is made up of many threads, one of which is economic class. Where the threads are woven together the different cultures act on behaviors of the individual and group. Of these rules, economic class is a surprisingly strong thread, one that is often overlooked—or at least minimized.

The additive model holds that:

- The hidden rules arise from the environment in which a person lives, that they help persons survive in the class in which they were raised. This means that the rules of class are not to be criticized, but that we simply add options, new rules, a wider range of responses, an ability to negotiate more environments. While these are framed as choices and not identity, any individuals who begin to work on achievements—such as economic stability, education, or getting sober—are changing their identity. How they make the transition is a choice: Will they stay connected with people from their past, or will they move into new circles? This is an individual and often painful choice/process. Being aware of the choice can smooth the process, whatever the decision.

- It is beneficial for middle-class people to learn the hidden rules of poverty—and not just so they're able to help people in poverty make changes, but because the hidden rules of poverty have value in their own right. Perhaps first among these is the value of relationships and the time given to them. The ability people in poverty have to establish quick but intimate relationships is an asset. In the additive model, change takes place, not just in the individual but in the theories of change and program designs of organizations. Middle-class organizations often have based their work on middle-class mindsets without an adequate mental model of poverty or knowledge of the hidden rules of the people they serve.

It is by adding to the hidden rules that one is raised with that people develop a range of responses that will give them control over their situations and open doors to new opportunities.

LANGUAGE ISSUES

The aha! Process approach calls for an extensive discussion of language issues, including definitions of the registers of language, discourse patterns, story structures, language experience in the first three years of life, cognitive issues, and strategies to deal with all of these. As a body of work, aha! Process's many books, workbooks, videos, classroom strategies, and program design strategies together make up a remarkable representation of the additive model. It is here that the model calls for an accurate naming of problems where the word *deficit* is used.

The additive model holds that:

- People build relationships by using the registers of language and discourse patterns skillfully.

- The strengths and uses of each register are encouraged where they can be most skillfully applied.

- Classroom interventions and agency strategies must be based on a clear understanding of the issues and a clear definition of the problems.

- The interventions themselves are built on the assets of the individual and the necessary changes fall as much on the professionals as on the individuals in poverty.

- Learning structures in the brain can be enhanced, but only by knowing the exact nature of the thinking that is occurring. In school settings the intervention cannot be random or general. The strategies offered by aha! Process are grade- and subject-specific.

- A rich language experience benefits children and prepares them for the world of work and school.

- Teachers value the language experience that children bring with them to school and prepare students to be able to skillfully navigate a wide range of language situations.

- In social service settings with adults, the additive model calls for the staff to become bilingual (able to translate from formal register to casual register).

- Change messages—be they about cardiovascular disease, breast feeding, birth weight, or the prevention of drug use—often taught in the formal register are now taught through a self-discovery process and by using mental models. Communication is meaningful and not just what Robert Sapolsky calls middle-class noise (Sapolsky, 1998).

FAMILY STRUCTURE

Matriarchal structure: All families have capabilities and strengths, and all families are faced with demands. In the course of life all families must face suffering and hard times, but some families seem to have more than their share of suffering to contend with. Under ordinary demands and stressors, families will become stronger as a result of their struggles. But there are some things that can overrun and overwhelm a family's capabilities; those include chronic addiction, mental illness, physical illness, and poverty (Henderson, 1996). People in poverty sometimes contend with more than poverty alone, and poverty itself is so stressful that there is a direct correlation between poverty and stress-related illnesses (Sapolsky, 1998). In high-demand conditions, families take on a structure that fits the survival needs of the family. In that context, the matriarchal structure and associated patterns of behavior are assets, but if viewed in light of a deficit model are often seen as negative or even as lacking in morals. A matriarchal family is not synonymous with a dysfunctional family. As in all economic classes, dysfunctional things may happen, but living in poverty does not equate with dysfunctional behaviors. The additive model provides an understanding and appreciation of matriarchal families and offers new information and ways of increasing resources.

The additive model holds that:

- Family structures evolve to meet the survival needs of the family and that they are strengths.

- As with aha! Process knowledge, awareness gives people optional ways to stabilize the chaotic circle of life, to envision new patterns and stories, to practice choice, and to build new resources.

SHARING AHA! PROCESS KNOWLEDGE
WITH ADULTS IN POVERTY

Co-investigation: Sharing aha! Process knowledge with people in poverty is done through a group investigation of the causes of poverty, examining the impact of poverty on the individual, and exploring new information. Individuals in the group assess their own resources and make plans to build their own future story. Here's one way of articulating the challenges faced by people in poverty:

Poverty traps people in the tyranny of the moment, making it very difficult to attend to abstract information or plan for the future (Freire, 1999; Sharron, 1996; Galeano, 1998)—the very things needed to build resources and financial assets. There are many causes of poverty, some having to do with the choices of the poor, but at least as many stemming from community conditions and political/economic structures (O'Connor, 2001; Brouwer, 1998; Gans, 1995).

The additive model holds that:

- People in poverty need an accurate perception of how poverty impacts them and an understanding of economic realities as a starting point both for reasoning and for developing plans for transition (Freire, 1999; Galeano, 1998).

- Using mental models for learning and reasoning, people can move from the concrete to the abstract (Freedman, 1996; Harrison, 2000; Sharron, 1996; Mattaini, 1993; Jaworski, 1996; Senge, 1994).

- People can be trusted to make good use of accurate information, presented in a meaningful way by facilitators who provide a relationship of mutual respect and act as co-investigators (Freire, 1999; Sapolsky, 1998; McKnight, 1995; Pransky, 1998; Farson, 1997).

- Using Ruby Payne's definition of the resources necessary for a full life, as well as her insights into the hidden rules of economic class, people can evaluate themselves and their situation, choose behaviors, and make plans to build resources (Miller, 2002).

- The community must provide services, support, and meaningful opportunities during transition and over the long term (Putnam, 2002; Kretzmann, 1993).

- In partnership with people from middle class and wealth, individuals in poverty can solve community and systemic problems that contribute to poverty (Phillips, 2002; Kretzmann, 1993).

AHA! PROCESS KNOWLEDGE
AND COMMUNITY SUSTAINABILITY

Community sustainability: This is an issue that all communities, states, and nations must now face. The world has seen several revolutionary changes: the change from hunter/gatherer societies to agriculture, the industrial revolution, the information age, and now the era in which we must determine how to use our resources and live in our environment—and yet retain vital resources for our children and grandchildren.

The mission of aha! Process—to directly impact the education and lives of individuals in poverty around the world—leads to a role in this revolution. Communities are awakening to the reality that they do not offer a sustainable way of life to their children and are looking for direction. Equity and critical mass impact the changes that are taking place. If a community allows any group to be disenfranchised for any reason (religion, race, class), the entire community becomes economically poorer (Sowell, 1998). When poverty reaches the point of critical mass in a community and efforts to reverse the problem don't succeed, the people with the most resources tend to move out of the community, leaving behind enclaves of poverty. At this point the community is no longer sustainable.

Responding to the impending crisis with the mindset that created it and with the strategies that have been used to address poverty to date is to invite more of the same results: more poverty and more communities at risk.

aha! Process defines community as any group that has something in common and the potential for acting together (Taylor-Ide 2002). The rich social capital that peaked in the post-World War II era—and that has been on the decline since—must be restored (Putnam, 2000). The barn-raising metaphor for communities where citizens contribute to the building of the barn with their particular skills, gifts, and talents must replace the vending-machine metaphor, which is currently in use. The vending-machine metaphor reduces community members to consumers or shoppers who put 75 cents into the machine expecting 75 cents of goods and services in return. With that mindset, it's no surprise that we find people kicking, shaking, and cursing the vending machine.

The additive model holds that:

- It's better to be a barn raiser than a consumer.

- All three classes must be at the table.

- Communities must have a shared understanding and a common vocabulary to build critical mass that is willing and motivated to make the necessary changes.

- Strategies must cover all the causes of poverty—from the behaviors of individuals to political/economic structures.

- Communities must build intellectual capital.

- Long-term plans of 20 to 25 years are needed.

- Quality-of-life indicators must be monitored and reported regularly in the same way that economic indicators are monitored and reported.

CONCLUSION

aha! Process offers a unique understanding of economic diversity that can give individual, families, and communities new ways of solving problems. It is the hope of aha! Process that 100 years from now poverty will no longer be viewed as economically inevitable. Two hundred years ago slavery was thought to be an economic necessity. It was not. One hundred fifty years ago it was believed that women were not capable of voting. That also was not true. We fervently hope that by 2100 individuals and society at large will no longer believe that poverty is inevitable. It is only by applying an additive model that we will understand and address both poverty and the underlying factors that have perpetuated it.

WORKS CITED

Andreas, Steve, & Faulkner, Charles. (Eds.) (1994). *NLP: The New Technology of Achievement.* New York, NY: Quill.

Bostrom, Meg. (2005). *Together for Success: Communicating Low-Wage Work as Economy, Not Poverty.* Ford Foundation Project. Douglas Gould & Co.

Brouwer, Steve. (1998). *Sharing the Pie: A Citizen's Guide to Wealth and Power in America.* New York, NY: Henry Holt & Company, Inc.

Comer, James P. (2001). Schools That Develop Children. *The American Prospect.* Volume 12. Number 7. April 23.

DeVol, Philip E. (2004). *Getting Ahead in a Just-Gettin'-by World: Building Your Resources for a Better Life.* Highlands, TX: aha! Process.

Farson, Richard. (1997). *Management of the Absurd: Paradoxes in Leadership.* New York, NY: Touchstone.

Freedman, Jill, & Combs, Gene. (1996). *Narrative Therapy: The Social Construction of Preferred Realities.* New York, NY: W.W. Norton & Company.

Freire, Paulo. (1999). *Pedagogy of the Oppressed.* New York, NY: Continuum Publishing Company.

Fussell, Paul. (1983). *Class: A Guide Through the American Status System.* New York, NY: Touchstone.

Galeano, Eduardo. (1998). *Upside Down: A Primer for the Looking-Glass World.* New York, NY: Metropolitan Books.

Gans, Herbert J. (1995). *The War Against the Poor.* New York, NY: Basic Books.

Harrison, Lawrence E., & Huntington, Samuel P. (Eds.). (2000). *Culture Matters: How Values Shape Human Progress.* New York, NY: Basic Books.

Henderson, Nan. (1996). *Resiliency in Schools: Making It Happen for Students and Educators.* Thousand Oaks, CA: Corwin Press.

Jaworski, Joseph. (1996). *Synchronicity: The Inner Path of Leadership.* San Francisco, CA: Berrett-Koehler Publishers.

Kahlenberg, Richard, D. (2001). Learning from James Coleman. *Public Interest.* Summer.

Kretzmann, John, & McKnight, John. (1993). *Building Communities From the Inside Out: A Path Toward Finding and Mobilizing a Community's Assets.* Chicago, IL: ACTA Publications.

Lewis, Oscar. (1966). The Culture of Poverty. *Scientific American.* Volume 215. Number 4. pp. 19–25.

Mattaini, Mark A. (1993). *More Than a Thousand Words: Graphics for Clinical Practice.* Washington, DC: NASW Press.

McKnight, John. (1995). *The Careless Society: Community and Its Counterfeits.* New York, NY: Basic Books.

Miller, William R., & Rollnick, Stephen. (2002). *Motivational Interviewing: Preparing People for Change,* Second Edition. New York, NY: Guilford Press.

O'Connor, Alice. (2001). *Poverty Knowledge: Social Science, Social Policy, and the Poor in Twentieth-Century U.S. History.* Princeton, NJ: Princeton University Press.

Payne, Ruby K., DeVol, Philip, & Dreussi Smith, Terie. (2001). *Bridges Out of Poverty: Strategies for Professionals and Communities.* Highlands, TX: aha! Process.

Phillips, Kevin. (2002). *Wealth and Democracy: A Political History of the American Rich.* New York, NY: Broadway Books.

Pransky, Jack. (1998). *Modello: A Story of Hope for the Inner-City and Beyond.* Cabot, VT: NEHRI Publications.

Putnam, Robert D. (2000). *Bowling Alone: The Collapse and Revival of American Community.* New York, NY: Simon & Schuster.

Sapolsky, Robert M. (1998). *Why Zebras Don't Get Ulcers: An Updated Guide to Stress, Stress-Related Diseases, and Coping.* New York, NY: W.H. Freeman & Company.

Sautter, Craig. (2005). Who Are Today's City Kids? Beyond the "Deficit Model." North Central Regional Educational Laboratory, a subsidiary of Learning Points Associates. http://www.ncrel.org/sdrs/cityschl/city1_1a.htm

Senge, Peter M. (1994). *The Fifth Discipline: The Art & Practice of The Learning Organization.* New York, NY: Currency Doubleday.

Sharron, Howard, & Coulter, Martha. (1996). *Changing Children's Minds: Feuerstein's Revolution in the Teaching of Intelligence.* Birmingham, England: Imaginative Minds.

Shipler, David K. (2004). *The Working Poor: Invisible in America.* New York, NY: Alfred A. Knopf.

Sowell, Thomas. (1998). Race, Culture and Equality. *Forbes.* October 5.

Sowell, Thomas. (1997). *Migrations and Cultures: A World View.* New York, NY: HarperCollins.

Taylor-Ide, Daniel, & Taylor, Carl, E. (2002). *Just and Lasting Change: When Communities Own Their Futures.* Baltimore, MD: Johns Hopkins University Press.

Washburne, Chandler. (1958). Conflicts Between Educational Theory and Structure. *Educational Theory.* Volume 8. Number 2. April.

■ ■ ■ ■

■ ■ ■ ■

Youngstown, Ohio, has had the unfortunate experience of living in the 'tyranny of the moment' for the last 35 years. Many local heroes have championed the cause of the poor in our area, but until we recognized the importance of having all economic classes at our planning table, we were just treading water in an increasingly large pool of poverty. Youngstown has become intentional about eliminating poverty on a communitywide level. Our courts, our businesses, our churches, our neighborhoods, and our individual citizens bring their voices to our planning table. Thanks to the guidance we've received on building a sustainable community, we have new thinking geared at solving old problems.

> **–Patricia Matthews,** Chair
> Mahoning County Bridges Out of Poverty Steering Committee
> Youngstown, Ohio

Before Getting Ahead I was trapped in a perpetual cycle of successive tyrannies of the moment! Obtaining the necessities and dealing with financial situations encompassed my life ... I couldn't see beyond my current circumstances. Through GA classes I was given the insight that explained why I was in poverty (as I was almost completely unaware) and how to champion it! I was in awe and shock when told that there are people (allies) in our community who care enough (I didn't think anyone cared) to invest their time in ME!! These allies have made a commitment to support me in furthering and sustaining my success (over a two-year period) for a better future! Amazing!!

> **–Carmella Montaro,** Women's Opportunity Center
> 2008 Getting Ahead Graduate
> Syracuse, New York

I was running on a treadmill, just running in place. It was hard to feed my son. I want to help myself and not always rely on family and friends. I am a man, and I am beginning to see myself in the future ... giving support to others, with work and being productive. Most people drag through their Mondays, but I look forward to seeing everyone in group, and I get excited. We should continue to do this work because then you find "diamonds in the rough" like me.

> **–Ams Baker,** Huntington Family Center
> 2008 Getting Ahead Graduate
> Syracuse, New York

AHA! PROCESS
DISASTER RECOVERY PLAN

Excerpted from *Bridges Out of Poverty*, 2006

When we become the victims of war and natural disasters or live in persistent poverty, we are impacted in these ways:

1. We are forced into the tyranny of the moment.

   a. Living in a broken world, we spend our time solving immediate, concrete problems.

   b. We lose our future orientation and, if the conditions persist, we lose our future stories.

2. We use reactive skills to survive. We are problem solvers.

   a. Reactive, problem-solving skills are needed in unstable and unpredictable environments.

   b. Proactive planning skills are possible when the environment is stabilized and the time horizon is months and years into the future.

3. We are taken advantage of.

   a. Stunned and preoccupied, we are unable to resist those who gather around disasters with the intent of profiting from the situation.

   b. We need immediate and concrete solutions and fall prey to those offering quick and easy answers. In this way we fall into debt and lose what property we may have.

c. We seek relief from stress and will spend some of what little money we have to lighten the day.

4. **We are disconnected from our social structures.**

   a. Our roles in society are disrupted.

   b. When others step in to make decisions without our input, we cannot rebuild our social structures.

5. **We who are in poverty are hit hardest.**

   a. We live in impoverished and vulnerable areas.

   b. We don't have the resources to escape.

   c. We are not at the planning table when disaster plans are being made.

   d. We are not at the planning table when recovery plans are being made.

   e. We aren't likely to take ownership of the plans created by others or feel accountable for them when we had no hand in making them.

   f. When we don't respond to the directions and suggestions of those who made the plans, we are accused of being dependent, unmotivated, and undeserving.

   g. We have learned that it is very hard to break out of poverty and build communities where everyone does well.

AHA! PROCESS, INC. CAN HELP BUILD A COMMUNITY WHERE EVERYONE CAN DO WELL. WE CAN:

1. **Assist people to break out of the tyranny of the moment and create their own future stories by:**

   a. Engaging people in examining the impact of the disaster on their community and themselves.

b. Assisting people to move from concrete thinking and reactive problem solving to abstract thinking and proactive problem solving.

c. Assisting people to make their own arguments for change and to find their own motivation.

2. **Engage people at the planning table with all sectors— government, business, civic, social services, investors, builders, and community-based organizations—by:**

a. Utilizing the concrete knowledge of those impacted by war, natural disaster, and poverty.

b. Inviting those impacted to join others in solving community problems and building prosperous communities.

3. **Provide a common language and shared constructs for all parties to use by:**

a. Developing a mental model for the community as it exists; define the reality.

b. Developing a mental model for the community's future story.

c. Defining the different environments in which community members live and the hidden rules of survival that arise from those environments.

d. Utilizing the hidden rules of survival to develop relationships of mutual respect and to resolve conflicts.

4. **Assist community-based organizations to develop sophisticated service delivery models to help people stabilize their home environments by:**

a. Assisting local service providers to develop a single plan with renters/homeowners for their personal housing, counseling, treatment, and safety needs.

b. Assisting the community to develop systemic approaches to overcome barriers to employment and stability, such as inadequate childcare, transportation, education, workforce skills, and safety.

c. Assisting educators to apply aha! Process constructs so children are provided with the best education possible.

5. **Assist the private sector to improve the retention rate of employees by:**

   a. Providing workshops for employers on aha! Process constructs.

   b. Providing training and consulting from community organizations that have applied aha! Process constructs to improve outcomes.

   c. Providing training and consulting from employers who have applied aha! Process constructs to improve retention rates.

6. **Assist in the development of a high-impact, community engagement model to create a prosperous and sustainable community by:**

   a. Creating a Steering Committee in the community to address all causes of poverty, including:

      i. Strategies to assist individuals in making good choices.

      ii. Strategies for the community to offer well-paying jobs, good healthcare, good education, and fair credit.

      iii. Strategies to protect renters/homeowners from predators and to develop alternatives to the "services" and products of predators.

      iv. Strategies that promote political and economic structures for wealth creation for all.

   b. Developing a national learning community made up of Bridges institutions and communities to create a number of models that can work in various settings.

AHA! PROCESS HAS THE PRODUCTS, PROCESSES, CONSULTANTS, AND PARTNERS, INCLUDING:

1. The book *Getting Ahead in a Just-Gettin'-By World*

   a. For those impacted, a 20-session, facilitator-led investigation into the impact of poverty/disasters on the individual and community using a workbook of the same title.

   b. Working in groups of 10–12, people will use the *Getting Ahead* workbook to:

      i. Do a self-assessment of their resources.

      ii. Do an assessment of their community.

      iii. Investigate economic realities, the hidden rules of class, and the change process as it applies to them.

      iv. Develop personal plans for their future stories.

      v. Prepare themselves to join the other community leaders at the planning table.

2. **Bridges Out of Poverty workshops are based on the book of the same title. The workshops provide the same constructs and language to community partners that Getting Ahead provides to those who have been impacted.**

3. *A Framework for Understanding Poverty,* **the seminal work of the innovator, Dr. Ruby K. Payne, and all the workshops and trainings associated with it, are available to educators.**

4. *Getting Ahead While Getting Out,* **a pre-release workbook based on** *Getting Ahead in a Just-Gettin'-By World* **for people returning from incarceration. The workbook is part of a**

complete Getting Out reentry model that provides support for returning citizens and their families for up to three years.

5. *The R Rules: A Guide for Teens to Identify and Build Resources,* a curriculum for teens that was designed to help students build life skills to manage the present and plan for a future in which everyone can live well.

6. *Bridges to Health and Healthcare,* a book that includes a continuum of policy and practice critical to improving health among people living in poverty, addressing both individual patient care and population health.

7. aha! Process champions, organizations, and communities that have applied aha! Process constructs successfully are available to assist employers, community-based organizations, and those who have been impacted to improve on-the-job performance, retention rates, and outcomes. These champions are from:

   a. Manufacturing

   b. Workforce development

   c. Family courts

   d. Schools

   e. Community colleges

   f. Communities at large

AHA! PROCESS HAS THE CAPACITY TO BEGIN WORKING ON PHASE I OF A PILOT PROJECT WITHIN FOUR WEEKS.

1. aha! Process would name a Team Leader for the initiative and would be available to participate in planning activities immediately.

2. aha! Process would work through a local contact to coordinate local resources and activities.

3. aha! Process will turn over the training and facilitator roles to local leaders as quickly as possible so they can conduct Bridges and Getting Ahead workshops.

4. Bridges Out of Poverty consultants and trainers can be scheduled to be in place as soon as four weeks.

5. Facilitators can be trained to conduct Getting Ahead workshops within six weeks.

6. A Steering Committee would be developed from people who have been through Getting Ahead and Bridges workshops who want to be part of the work.

7. Phase II of the pilot would include:

   a. Community-based organizations, service delivery model development

   b. Workforce development training and consulting

   c. Employer-based training and consulting

   d. Health and healthcare training and consulting

TO LEARN MORE, CONTACT:

> **aha! Process, Inc.**
> **P.O. Box 727**
> **Highlands, TX 77562**
> **Tel: (800) 424-9484**
>
> **www.ahaprocess.com**

■ ■ ■ ■

Since 1997 a total of 182 participants have graduated from our Buck County Opportunity Council's Economic Self-Sufficiency (ES) Program and eliminated their need for government welfare subsidies, such as TANF, food stamps, and subsidized housing. The Council has incorporated the Getting Ahead curriculum into its ES Program, which is the starting point for all motivated, hard-working persons who aspire to implement their personal plans that lead to self-sufficiency and ultimately a more secure economic future.

Equally, the Bridges Out of Poverty training informs and enhances our Council's mission and equips staff and community with the best understanding of how to assist low-income people to facilitate responsible, self-directed decision making, planning, and ultimately self-sufficiency. After reviewing literally hundreds of tools, we believe that Getting Ahead and Bridges Out of Poverty are significant additions to our long-term work to help people permanently leave poverty.

–Tammy B. Schoonover, ACSW, LSW, Director of Training
Bucks County Opportunity Council, Inc.
Doylestown, Pennsylvania

For generations, various groups and agencies have dedicated their efforts to the reduction of poverty's impact on the poor. Not only are the poor still with us, their struggle seems to be getting harder. Next steps require that we come together to integrate community efforts, bringing business, faith, social services, government, and policy together with the persons our efforts impact, to create and test new approaches to viable solutions. Bridges constructs have given Community Properties of Ohio the tools to build relationships with over 25 (and growing) community agencies. Our community conversations have had an impact on employment, payday lending legislation, suspended license driving privileges, healthy food access, and more. Those of use at the table are beginning to see a new day coming for generationally poor families. Our community is on its way to saying, "Remember when …"

–Louise R. Seipel, Director
Community Properties Impact Corporation
Columbus, Ohio

■■■■5

BUILDING BRIDGES COMMUNITIES

First published at www.ahaprocess.com in 2008

BRIDGES OUT OF POVERTY MODEL—PART I

The Bridges Out of Poverty Model is based on the following books and papers:

- *Bridges Out of Poverty: Strategies for Professionals and Communities*
- *Getting Ahead in a Just-Gettin'-By World: Building Your Resources for a Better Life*
- Additive Model: the aha! Process Approach to Building Sustainable Communities
- Using the Hidden Rules of Class to Create Sustainable Communities
- aha! Process Platform for Economic Justice

BRIDGES ENGAGES ORGANIZATIONS AND COMMUNITIES IN THE FOLLOWING PROCESSES:

- Community members attend Bridges workshops where they:
  - Develop mental models of the environments of poverty, middle class, and wealth
  - Examine the causes of poverty

- ▫ Begin to understand how the differing environments can produce different hidden rules of class

- ▫ Define resources that are necessary for a high quality of life and explore community action and policies that can enhance resources

- ▫ Explore how the information can be used to create relationships between and among classes so that all can participate in solving problems at the community and systemic levels

- People in poverty participate in Getting Ahead work groups to examine the impact of poverty on themselves and their communities, investigate class and race issues as they apply to poverty and the creation of wealth, complete a self-assessment of resources, evaluate their communities, and develop plans for personal and community prosperity.

- Service providers attend workshops to enhance front-line staff skills and improve program designs.

- Communities:

  - ▫ Organize to address poverty issues in the broadest way

  - ▫ Support organizations that assist people in poverty to stabilize their environments and build resources

  - ▫ Enhance service delivery systems to provide long-term support for people making the transition out of poverty

  - ▫ Develop community engagement models that support transition and address all causes of poverty

THE BRIDGES OUT OF POVERTY MODEL HAS THESE FEATURES:

- Economic class is used as an analytical category to understand and address poverty. There are many lenses through which poverty can be examined. aha! Process primarily offers the lens of economic class. Communities that utilize the Bridges model share a lexicon that facilitates change.

- Mental models of economic class are used to describe, compare, and contrast the environments of poverty, middle class, and wealth. Knowledge of the hidden rules that arise from those environments is used to promote understanding, resolve conflicts, and improve the design of programs and policies.

- Bridges constructs are transformational for people from all classes. This work encourages all participants to explore, understand, and own the way they experience the advantages and disadvantages of life in the U.S. This deepens our understanding of how poverty impacts everyone and directs us to the changes we need to make in our own sphere.

- People in poverty are understood to be problem solvers. Their knowledge and insights about poverty and the community are needed to develop meaningful plans. Communities that utilize the Bridges model have people in poverty actively engaged with others at the decision-making level.

- Research on the causes of poverty is framed into four clusters that embrace all points of view. Those clusters are: behaviors of the individual, human and social capital in the community, exploitation of people in poverty, and political/economic structures. Using this research encourages people of all classes, races, and political persuasions to participate in the dialogue about poverty. Communities that utilize the Bridges model are intentional about developing strategies to cover all four clusters of research.

- Bringing people together across class lines creates energy for change. Changes take place at the individual, organizational, and community levels. Once people form relationships of mutual respect, they are much less likely to abandon each other. Organizations that utilize the Bridges model are accountable to their customers. Communities that utilize the Bridges model are committed to building social capital and prosperous, healthy communities for all.

- Some organizations and communities that utilize the Bridges model become champions, which is to say their ownership of Bridges knowledge, coupled with the best practices of their own field or discipline, make them a learning center for others. Some champions are conducting independent research that will eventually enhance the transfer of knowledge to others who are committed to ending poverty.

- Partnerships: Bridges has been developing partnerships between and among organizations that are committed to ending poverty. Bridges is exploring partnerships with organizations that address systemic racism. Most organizations and communities seem more willing to address poverty through the lens of economic class than the lens of racism. Communities that utilize the Bridges model are urged to continue their work on poverty by addressing systemic racism. aha! Process offers a 30-minute video from Jodi Pfarr in which she shares her thinking on the complexities of where poverty intersects with ageism, racism, sexism, able-bodyism, and other "isms."

Evaluation: Bridges encourages all Bridges and Getting Ahead sites and communities to collect data on program outcomes. There are two national providers that can help build community data-collection systems and report on outcomes.

Charity Tracker PLUS offers a cloud-based evaluation tool to assess Getting Ahead effectiveness and track usage of community resources. Communities can track model fidelity, stability, resource development, and return on investment (ROI) elements embedded in case management.

MPOWR offers web-based case management and community collaboration tools. Clients who receive services from several organizations can have a single case plan instead of a separate plan at each organization. In addition, MPOWR can provide outcomes for Getting Ahead graduates, including information on stability, resource development, and ROI.

BRIDGES OUT OF POVERTY MODEL—PART II
HOW TO DEVELOP
A BRIDGES COMMUNITY: STEPS

Communities engage in building a Bridges Community because people are attracted to Bridges constructs and because they want to live in sustainable communities. Building a Bridges Community tends to be organic and messy, not unlike gardening. It's not linear or mechanical like building a house. Every community has its own leaders, history, circumstances, and best practices and will go about building a Bridges Community in its own way. There are, however, some principles and steps that we've learned from other Bridges Communities that can help guide the work.

Please note that an assumption is being made that readers are familiar with Bridges constructs through reading or attendance at a workshop.

GUIDING PRINCIPLES

We know that the actions we take will result in changes at the individual, community, and systemic levels.

People in all three classes will be challenged to think and behave differently in their personal lives, at work, and as community members.

At the community level, organizations will be challenged to rethink the design of their programs, collaboratives will smooth the pathway for people who use their services, and communities will protect its members from predators. The business sector will be challenged to improve retention rates and move employees to better-paying jobs. The whole community will be encouraged to become engaged in ending poverty.

The growing number of people engaged in developing a sustainable community will result in a movement that can effectively address systemic issues. Guided by the experience and knowledge of people who are making the transition out of poverty, the community will know what changes are needed at the agency, city, county, state, and federal levels.

THE BRIDGES MODEL IS DRIVEN BY THE FOLLOWING GUIDING PRINCIPLES:

Bring all classes and races to the decision-making table

- Come together to solve problems.

- Talk *with* people—not at them, to them, or for them.

Bring all sectors to the table

- The sectors include: government, social, private/business, civic, community-based, and faith-based.

- Every sector is needed; add new sectors over time.

- Each sector plays a vital role; for example, the business sector creates financial wealth, something the other sectors cannot do.

Bring all political persuasions to the table

- Provide a dialogue about poverty and prosperity that transcends "either/or" and addresses community sustainability in a meaningful way.

- Solve concrete local problems.

Stabilize the environment and build resources

- Poverty is defined as the degree to which a person does without resources, so building resources is a key goal of a Bridges Community.

- It's easier to build resources if the daily experience and environment of people in poverty are stabilized.

- It takes individual, family, and community action to build resources.

Address all causes of poverty

- The Bridges Community must take the most inclusive approach and be intentional about addressing all causes of poverty.

- It's much harder to address political/economic structures than it is to address the individual, thus the need to be intentional.

- The Community Sustainability Grid is a concrete approach to all causes of poverty, as well as a planning tool.

Provide long-term support for transition

- The greater the disparity in income and wealth, the harder it is to get out of poverty.

- The middle class and working poor are in trouble too, and the number of people in poverty is growing. It's going to get harder to get people out of poverty and build prosperous communities during the next few years.

- Current U.S. policies pull supports away as people begin moving out of poverty, just when they need the supports the most.

- Communities will need to build supports to mitigate "cliff effects"—and to advocate for sound policies.

- Engage people in poverty to guide the work of overcoming obstacles and designing new partnerships and approaches.

Create a sustainable community

- All communities are challenged to pass on a high quality of life to following generations.

- People in poverty must be included in who "counts" as part of the community.

- Ensure that the goal is to create a prosperous, healthy, sustainable community where everyone does well.

ORGANIZATIONAL PRINCIPLES

Everyone owns it, and no one owns it

- Bridges Communities often start with the work of one person or organization that takes ownership and responsibility for moving things ahead. That's a necessary thing.

- But … if the ownership stays with one organization for too long, the initiative will become identified with that organization and will live or die by its reputation and longevity. In addition, others who like the work may become "outsiders" to planning and development.

- Eventually the expansion of a Bridges initiative will require widening the net beyond what any one organization can provide.

- All participants should own the Bridges constructs within their own sphere of influence and control. Another way of saying this: Apply the concepts where you are—in your life or organization—before asking others to apply them.

- When a number of agencies decide to use Bridges, sophisticated service delivery models can be developed.

- Most Bridges Communities eventually decide that the whole community is needed to help people get out of poverty. Developing a high-impact community engagement model is the next task.

Don't wait for authorization to act

- Coming together to solve community problems is an American tradition.

- Working in "silos" often slows action or puts organizations at cross-purposes.

- A participatory democracy is when everyone's voice is heard—when people come together to solve problems.

Transparency

- Clarify roles and decision-making boundaries in order to establish trust.

- Transparency in decision making, money management, planning, reporting writing, publicity, and intention are necessary.

STEPS FOR DEVELOPING A BRIDGES COMMUNITY ... NOT NECESSARILY IN THIS ORDER

1. Introduce Bridges constructs

a. The first people to learn about Bridges are typically those who work in organizations that interact closely with people in poverty: government services, schools, social services, healthcare, community-based organizations, law enforcement, and so on. Usually the interest grows by word of mouth, and more workshops are planned.

b. In every community there is group of people who catch the idea that Bridges constructs can be used at the community level. They are the driving force behind Bridges.

c. Working with others who are attracted to the work, they organize and fund follow-up workshops: Applying the Concepts, Design/Redesign, Getting Ahead facilitator trainings, and more.

d. As the idea grows, so does the work; it takes time and money to get things from the informational stage to the collaboration stage.

e. These people are visionaries with the connections, credibility, and ability to get things done. Bridges Communities happen because of them.

2. Develop critical mass

a. There is a tipping point at which Bridges constructs become the lexicon for understanding poverty and prosperity. Communities achieve critical mass by:

- ▫ Hosting Bridges workshops for people and organizations that interact with people in poverty regularly

- ▫ Providing short Bridges sessions for businesses, local leaders, board members, and administrators who cannot attend day-long sessions

- ▫ Doing follow-up study groups and book clubs—and by applying the concepts at the personal and agency level

- ▫ Developing a stable of Certified Bridges Trainers to train, reinforce the concepts, and deepen the utilization of the constructs

b. Groups and organizations that interact with people in poverty, but not to the degree of those that first learn about Bridges, are typically the next to attend workshops: faith-based groups, civic organizations, foundations, and more businesses.

c. The community at large is informed about Bridges by word of mouth and through typical media campaigns and events.

d. The ownership of Bridges shifts to the community as people and organizations begin teaching the constructs and changing their own ways of being.

3. Offer Getting Ahead to people in poverty

a. Making Bridges information available to people in poverty must be done early so that the organizers are talking with people in poverty, not about them or for them.

b. Getting Ahead is crucial to the development of a Bridges Community because it directly engages people in poverty and requires support from the community.

c. Providing access to Bridges information to people in poverty energizes the whole process and points to the next things that must be done to help people get out of poverty.

d. Organizing Getting Ahead sessions involves:

- Selecting and training a stable of facilitators who are familiar with Bridges constructs and have the "characteristics" of Getting Ahead facilitators as defined in that work

- Recruiting participants, called "investigators"

- Finding a location where the group can meet

- Securing the funds to pay the investigators and cover the cost of incidentals

e. The Bridges Community must bring Getting Ahead graduates to the table to help inform the group on:

- The true nature of poverty in the community

- The barriers to getting out of poverty

- Their assessment of the community

- Their solutions

f. Getting Ahead makes it possible for people to come together to solve community problems and build prosperous communities.

4. Develop an organizational structure, including a Steering Committee

a. Start with those who share a vision, then add members as they are attracted to the Bridges work. It takes no prescribed number of organizations to start a Steering Committee. Two things build the numbers: working toward critical mass by exposing people to the ideas and taking action. Some examples:

- Running Getting Ahead groups

- Addressing predatory lending practices

- Helping to stabilize the environment with revolving loans, as well as access to good cars at a fair cost

- Helping to build resources by providing Individual Development Accounts and working with the business sector on retention issues and opportunities to well-paying jobs

b. Have an aha! Process consultant facilitate a Community Sustainability Workshop to explore options and learn how other communities have structured their Bridges work.

- Attend Bridges Institutes where Bridges Communities meet to share ideas and best practices.

- Visit the aha! Process website to listen to taped Bridges Community conference calls on such a variety of topics as reentry from incarceration, employers, health and healthcare, youth, college, legal, and building collaboratives.

c. Establish the purpose of the Steering Committee. Some examples:

- To address all causes of poverty

- To create a prosperous community where everyone does well

- To help people get out of poverty by stabilizing the environment and building resources

- To support people during their transition out of poverty

- To utilize the strengths of all members and all sectors to achieve the goals of the group

- To build a sophisticated service delivery system

- To develop a community engagement approach

d. The structure should ensure that:

- There is a safe place for impartial exploration of views and opinions, where people are involved in action

- The group is guided by and adheres to the Bridges Model and guiding principles

- There is a commitment to shared power and respect for minority opinions; consider a consensus-based approach to decision making

- Meetings are about planning, action, problem solving, next steps, deliberation, collaborative solutions, celebrations, and learning; they should not be about "updating" one another

- No single organization "owns" Bridges but that every organization and person has ownership

□ Action is assured, but it is not predetermined or prescribed

□ The work is driven by practice more than theory

□ All groups can get support for the Bridges work being done at their organization

e. Various organizations can serve as fiscal or administrative agents for grants that are awarded to members of the Bridges community.

□ Work can be done in both large and small groups

□ Records are kept of Bridges events, Getting Ahead activities, and the history of the work

□ Quality-improvement activities, evaluations, and research can be conducted

□ Actions are coordinated

f. The following Bridges Community Model depicts the relationships, roles, and actions of a fully developed Bridges community.

DEVELOPING A BRIDGES COMMUNITY

Purpose and Functions of a Bridges Steering Committee

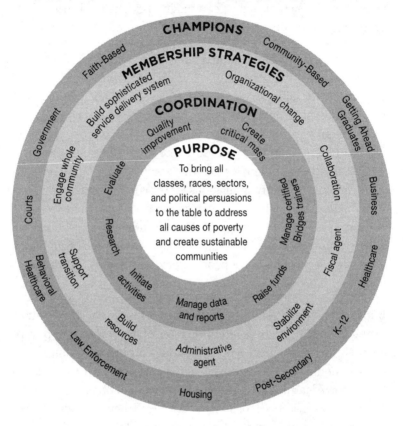

This mental model derives from the experience of a number of communities that formed Bridges Steering Committees. It describes common features and the general functions of those Steering Committees. While it is not prescriptive, it can give new communities a way to examine aspects of the work that others have identified.

The inner circle should describe the purpose or shared understanding that brings people together to do Bridges work, whatever that is.

The ring labeled "Coordination" honors the work of the people and/or organizations that take responsibility for getting things started. Typically that means conducting Bridges workshops, but it grows to include the other functions listed in the circle.

The "Membership" takes on broader aspects of the work and guides the activities of the coordinator, but each member organization is responsible for taking action at various levels. First, it should look to how Bridges can be applied to its own policies, procedures, and programs. It also might seek funds to support the internal work it does or collaborative initiatives it takes with other members. It might serve as an administrative/fiscal agent for a particular project, say, running Getting Ahead or doing poverty simulations for the community. Another level would be to work with other organizations to develop a better service delivery system that will support the transition of people in poverty. The organization might be situated to engage other sectors in Bridges work, say, elected officials or people from the business sector.

Some communities have Bridges "champions"—a judge who uses Bridges constructs to improve outcomes in family court, a manufacturing firm that improves retention rates of new hires from poverty, or healthcare providers who help their employees stabilize their environments and move toward better-paying jobs. Organizations that become learning centers for others are called Bridges champions. They have taken Bridges constructs, have added their own best practices and theories, and have developed new and vital knowledge.

A Bridges Steering Committee is about application and action. There is no limit to the creativity of the communities that take on this work.

Bridges Steering Committees can serve as the foundation for at least four areas of action. In the communities that have gone ahead, we see patterns emerging in this sequence. The sequence follows the path of people in poverty as they work their way out of poverty. It's important to note that this is informed by people in poverty. The following mental model shows the four areas of action as they arise from the foundational work of the Bridges Steering Committee.

DEVELOPING A BRIDGES COMMUNITY
Purpose and Functions of a Bridges Steering Committee

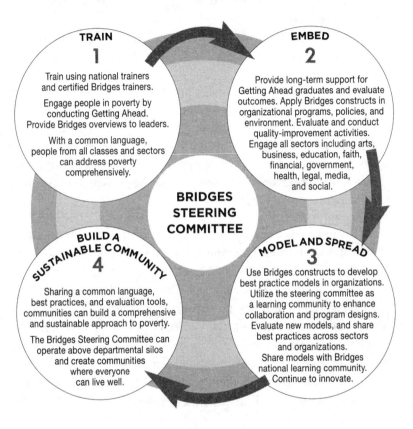

TRAIN

1

Train using national trainers and certified Bridges trainers.

Engage people in poverty by conducting Getting Ahead. Provide Bridges overviews to leaders.

With a common language, people from all classes and sectors can address poverty comprehensively.

EMBED

2

Provide long-term support for Getting Ahead graduates and evaluate outcomes. Apply Bridges constructs in organizational programs, policies, and environment. Evaluate and conduct quality-improvement activities. Engage all sectors including arts, business, education, faith, financial, government, health, legal, media, and social.

BRIDGES STEERING COMMITTEE

BUILD A SUSTAINABLE COMMUNITY

4

Sharing a common language, best practices, and evaluation tools, communities can build a comprehensive and sustainable approach to poverty.

The Bridges Steering Committee can operate above departmental silos and create communities where everyone can live well.

MODEL AND SPREAD

3

Use Bridges constructs to develop best practice models in organizations. Utilize the steering committee as a learning community to enhance collaboration and program designs. Evaluate new models, and share best practices across sectors and organizations. Share models with Bridges national learning community. Continue to innovate.

Training

Exposure to Bridges concepts almost always begins before the development of a Bridges Steering Committee and continues long after the committee is formed. Changing mindsets is the highest order of change. Once that occurs, many new approaches to poverty become possible. In every community there is a catalyst: Someone is attracted to the concepts and wants to share the information with their organization or the community at large. Training is generally provided by aha! Process national trainers or by a licensed site. The number of trainings depends in part on the size of the community.

One or two visits may be enough in small communities, and 6–10 may be necessary in cities. People have to hear the ideas and decide if they like them before they will commit themselves to the work. Ideally the catalyst will gather information from the audience about their interest in Bridges so that everyone who is attracted will be entered in a database and can be engaged as the initiative develops.

Developing a team of certified Bridges trainers is important because the ownership of the ideas must shift from the experts at aha! Process to the soon-to-be experts in the community. The role of the certified trainers is to expose as many people as possible to the ideas and encourage them to take ownership of the ideas too. Without that, it will be impossible to embed and use the ideas at the individual, institutional, or community level.

During this phase, a Bridges Steering Committee or another collaborative is often formed. One role of the committee is to recruit, train, and support certified Bridges trainers. They also need to assure that CEOs, executive directors, boards of directors, and other community leaders are trained. Trainers must cover many sectors: health, criminal justice, employers, and education—from pre-K to postsecondary—to name a few. aha! Process offers special certifications for a number of sectors. Experience tells us that training must be ongoing to reduce turnover in employment and to deepen the understanding of Bridges through application of the concepts.

Effective training includes recruiting and training facilitators for Getting Ahead and making that program available to people in poverty. Getting Ahead is an energy-producing action that brings people in poverty to the planning and decision-making tables of the community. Their insights and knowledge of poverty and the barriers they face will make it possible for the Bridges Steering Committee to do relevant work.

Embed

The focus now is for each organization to embed the concepts in their way of doing business. The assumption is that the front-line staff and management will use the new insights to improve their relationships and interactions with people from other economic classes. But changes may need to be made in procedures, program design, policies, and in the environment; in other words, institutional change must occur. Without this step, Bridges will die on the vine as have many other professional development programs.

Bridges has a number of tools that will assist redesign teams, but there is no single solution that is imposed on Bridges sites. If that were the case, if Bridges were to provide "the answer," we might not see the variety of brilliant ideas that arise from those who take up the challenge to innovate in their own settings.

One exercise from the private sector, titled "Examining the Client Life Cycle" and first described in *Bridges Out of Poverty,* has proven to be a good starting place. Many processes and activities clients experience when they walk through our doors are inadvertently disrespectful and therefore ineffective. "Examining the Client Life Cycle" leverages what we now know about class differences to find parts of our processes we can improve.

The same activity can be used to examine clients' experiences with all the organizations they access in the community.

While embedding Bridges constructs, it is helpful if everyone is viewed as a co-creator. This includes the clients (people in poverty), front-line staff, supervisors, middle managers, and top management. Co-creation requires that people play three roles and be willing to change roles. A person may be in the creator role now but later be a challenger or a coach. It takes different types of thinking to innovate.

The first to provide information about current practices can be Getting Ahead graduates. While in Getting Ahead, they investigate how organizations approach change and then conduct an assessment of the community. Their insights into barriers and effective programming are based on their concrete experiences and knowledge. This unique feature of Bridges is based on the understanding that people in poverty are problem-solvers. Without their input, our work would not be nearly as relevant or successful.

Some individuals and organizations become champions. By that we mean their success is so compelling that others naturally seek them out to learn more. In Bridges we are intentional about identifying and supporting champions within organizations and within communities. Making room for champions to meet and interact can result in amazing breakthroughs. Some of these stories are captured in the *From Vision to Action* series. These collections of best practices, published by aha! Process, contain stories that have been reviewed and selected by peers.

Model and spread

Creating models that can be replicated or adapted is the next step in the creative process. These models are a natural outgrowth of the learning community. New Bridges sites are moving quickly from their first Bridges trainings to presenting at the Addressing the Challenges of Poverty annual conference. It has been done in as few as three years. This is only possible because the learning is spreading from organization to organization, site to site, state to state, and across sectors.

The annual conference, where most of the sessions are provided by practitioners, is not the only way the aha! Process and Bridges communities can help one another and develop new sites. Other activities include teleconferences, webinars, site visits, social media, websites, newsletters, regional conferences, and contributing articles to the next edition of *From Vision to Action.*

Build a sustainable community

Bridges Communities take the long view; they are looking 20 and 25 years down the road, knowing that building communities where everyone can live well is a big future story. Sustainability begins with little steps like getting past the one- and two-year funding and planning cycle. It's also important to get above the departmental silos that pit one organization against another for local funding during hard times. Bridges needs to be deeply rooted in the community; it cannot be another brilliant but short-lived idea that comes and goes with the CEO, executive director, or superintendent.

In Bridges we must be intentional about these things:

- Sharing a common language and mindset about poverty so that when boards are searching for a new executive director, they expect the incoming person to learn and maintain fidelity to the Bridges model.

- Using a common data-collection system to report on outcomes as parts of a collaborative. A shared data and reporting system can stitch a collaborative together.

- Choosing policies that: bring people in poverty into stable working and living conditions; build the 11 resources through individual, institutional, and community change; and build social capital and social coherence so that all people are heard and valued.

- A sustainable initiative is needed to build a sustainable community.

SUPPORT FROM AHA! PROCESS

Training

- Bridges workshops of all lengths; introduction to the core concepts for all sectors

- Applying the Concepts; skills and strategies for front-line staff

- Bridges Out of Poverty Trainer Certification

- Getting Ahead facilitator training; Getting Ahead while Getting Out Facilitator Certification

- Bridges to Health and Healthcare workshops and trainer certification

- Law-enforcement workshops

- Workshops based on the book *What Every Church Member Should Know About Poverty*

Consulting

- Design/Redesign; organizational change

- Sustainable Communities; moving toward Bridges Communities

Materials

- *Bridges Out of Poverty*

- *Bridges* workbook

- *Getting Ahead in a Just-Gettin'-By World;* for people in poverty

- *Getting Ahead While Getting Out;* a reentry model

- *Tactical Communication,* first responder edition

- *The R Rules;* for young people

- *From Vision to Action vols. I and II;* best practices from Bridges Communities

- *DVDs: Jodi's Stories, Intersection of Poverty and the 'Isms'*

- *Bridges Out of Poverty Audio Workshop* download: Jodi Pfarr's two-day Bridges training

aha! Process website (www.ahaprocess.com)

- Best-practices page for Bridges Communities

- Free monthly webinars

- Free monthly newsletter

- Free downloads and video clips

- Bridges Community phone conferences; recorded sessions for all to hear

Bridges Institutes

- Build on the community of practice that is developing in the U.S.

- Addressing the Challenges of Poverty national conference held annually; Bridges champions share information and best practices.

- People in poverty are included at all Bridges Institutes.

Evaluation and research

- Agencies and communities that conduct evaluations will be encouraged to share results.

- Charity Tracker PLUS: cloud-based evaluation tools to assess Getting Ahead effectiveness, www.charity-tracker.com.

- MPOWR: Web-based case management and community collaboration tools, www.mpowr.com.

- Getting Ahead mobile app: daily personal support for Getting Ahead graduates' stability and resource development, www.beaconvoice.com.

As has been noted throughout, there is no prescription for how to end poverty or build a prosperous community using Bridges constructs. This paper identifies what we have learned so far. But poverty and community sustainability are only two parts of the puzzle we face. We need to be aware of the interlocking nature of all the problems. This is a very creative time for people who are part of social justice, economic justice, sustainability, environmental, and indigenous movements. Innovations will come from the ground up in those movements too, so the learning environment is as limitless as the strategies and solutions that you create in your community.

Those who have already developed Bridges Communities and Steering Committees are willing to help others on the journey. We only ask that as your community moves ahead you also share what you learn with the rest of us.

■ ■ ■ ■

■ ■ ■ ■

Here at Youngstown State University, an urban research university in the heart of the aftermath of "Big Steel," the concepts and practical strategies described in this book have been put to work. Like so many communities, this region already had a legacy of generational poverty, but the collapse of the steel industry in 1984, coupled with the absence of competing interests, sentenced yet another wave of residents, tied to place, into a new generation of poverty.

Phil DeVol's ideas have provided our students/clients/customers, along with our institutions/agencies/churches, with two critical factors for change. The first is new insight into one another's mindsets and lives, which allows respectful relationships to develop—and gets people to listen and hear and understand in new ways what they thought they once knew. The importance of this cannot be overemphasized. The second is a continuum of strategies and work to be done that gives everyone a place at the table. The practice of inclusion also cannot be overemphasized.

We are using DeVol's work in the micro-community of the YSU campus and helping other post-secondary institutions do the same. Our region is using this work—and drawing on the network of other communities for wisdom and ideas. It isn't easy, but it is exciting and fundamentally different from anything we've seen or done before. This latest book brings DeVol's newest writings under one cover and will be helpful to communities looking for effective strategies to end poverty.

–Karla Krodel, Director
Metro Credit Education Outreach
Youngstown State University
Youngstown, Ohio

Having trained adult-to-adult mentors for many years, Bridges to Sustainable Communities is the best and most comprehensive tool I have found to be effective and cause change. I have struggled to find all the pieces to get clients started on the road to self-sufficiency, maintain throughout the journey, and finally arrive at resiliency. Bridges is the tool that connects all stages of the journey. This model transcends social classes and unites the community in one common goal: ending poverty. It is proactive and extremely effective.

–Michelle Kempema, Director
Family Resources
Greeley, Colorado

▪▪▪▪6

WHOLE SYSTEM PLANNING
Developing the mindset, models, structures, and tools to take Bridges work to a higher level

First published here in 2009

This paper is a challenge to Bridges Steering Committees— a challenge to raise the level of our work. We have the mindset, models, structures, and tools to help invent communities where *everyone* can live well; all that's missing is an *intention* to do more, to be of even *more* help.

In this paper we will:

- Review our history.

- Consider what we already have to offer our communities.

- Explore how to use a new tool, the Bridges Continuum.

- Identify barriers to change at the organizational and community level.

- Discuss how we can do whole system planning.

- Sharpen our focus on the metrics and goals that really matter.

A BRIEF HISTORY OF 'BRIDGES'

We've learned a lot since *Bridges Out of Poverty* was first published in 1999. We learned from a number of individuals, organizations, and communities that applied our ideas. Ten years have produced new books, such as my *Getting Ahead in a Just-Gettin'-By World;* Jodi Pfarr's book for police titled *Tactical Communication;* Elizabeth Souther's *The R Rules* for teens; and *Understanding and Engaging*

Under-Resourced College Students by Karen Becker, Karla Krodel, and Bethanie Tucker.

The first major application and successful use of Bridges ideas came from Cascade Engineering (CE), a plastics firm in Grand Rapids, Michigan. The success was documented by James Bradley in case studies published by Cornell University and by Stanford University's *Social Innovations Review.* The CE account sparked other innovations in the business sector and fired the imaginations of thousands of people who heard the story.

People in more than 50 cities and counties in the United States have taken ownership of Bridges and are applying comprehensive, high-impact strategies to help people make the transition out of poverty. There are 1,300 certified Bridges trainers and eight licensed Bridges sites. The community of practice is growing as new sites are added—and the older sites offer their best practices at annual Bridges Institutes.

The St. Joseph County Bridges Out of Poverty Initiative (South Bend, Indiana) was the first 501(c)(3) with a full-time director and is now a licensed Bridges site. There is broad community support for the initiative, and more than 600 people have participated in the Bridges Day One training. Elected officials (both Republicans and Democrats) hosted a meeting of business leaders and social service providers in support of the Future Story Project, which is designed to employ Getting Ahead graduates. Getting Ahead has been implemented at 11 sites in St. Joseph County and has produced more than 200 graduates. One of those sites, the YWCA of St. Joseph County, has had its Bridges program receive the National YWCA Hallmark Award as the outstanding employment initiative for the year.

The Menominee Nation in Keshena, Wisconsin, has put together the most complete poverty initiative using aha! Process strategies and tools. aha! Process is the Texas-based company behind Getting Ahead and Bridges. Trainings based on the books *A Framework for Understanding Poverty* and *Bridges Out of Poverty* were followed up with deeper work in schools and community organizations. The Wisconsin community is using the books *Getting Ahead in a Just-Gettin'-By World*, *Reading by Age 5*, *Collaboration For Kids*, and *The R Rules*.

In Eastern Slovakia, where one paper included in this book was translated into Slovak, a Bridges initiative to bring about systemic change is being developed. One European Union grant has been awarded; another two are being sought.

Getting Ahead graduates are becoming influential at many levels: teaching Bridges constructs to Juvenile Services staff in West Virginia; working with housing developers in Gulfport, Mississippi; participating on the Governor's Anti-Poverty Task Force in Ohio; speaking to legislators about predatory lending practices; assisting with the implementation of Bridges in the colleges of Education and Social Services at Youngstown State University in Ohio.

Getting Ahead is being used at more than 100 sites and has been translated into Spanish and Slovak. The Getting Ahead Network website (www.gettingaheadnetwork.com) gives community leaders, facilitators, and investigators a place to share stories, documents, and best practices.

The initiative in Syracuse, New York, trained approximately 90 certified Bridges trainers and 16 Getting Ahead facilitators before running into organizational and financial problems. For a year certified Bridges trainers provided workshops and Getting Ahead without pay before they received a cash flow commitment of over half million dollars for two years.

Getting Ahead is producing encouraging results. Of 312 Getting Ahead graduates in Mahoning and Trumbull counties in Ohio, full-time employment increased from 31% to 76%—and 58% enrolled in postsecondary education. Of the 58 graduates at the YWCA in South Bend, Indiana, 84% increased income, 69% moved toward educational goals, 63% found employment, and 84% improved their support system. In numerous site visits with Getting Ahead graduates, it has become apparent that Getting Ahead graduates are much more likely to become independent, self-directed, and focused on their future stories than to become "compliant" employees or clients. In the criminal justice system, the Family Court in Fort Wayne, Indiana, has been a champion almost as long as Cascade Engineering. For a number of years, Judge Charles Pratt has been conducting workshops on the Family Court model he developed with aha! Process constructs.

The Specialized Dockets Section of the Supreme Court of Ohio took an interest in Bridges and began sending judges and others to become certified Bridges trainers. Judge Jennifer Brunner's Franklin County Drug Court was the first in the nation to offer Getting Ahead to drug court participants. When Judge Brunner was elected Secretary of State for Ohio, she implemented a social health index called Better Lives, Better Ohio (www.sos.state.oh.us). Secretary Brunner learned about the social health index while at a Certified Bridges Trainer event. She contracted with aha! Process for assistance in developing Better Lives, Better Ohio. The Supreme Court of Ohio is now implementing a four-year, four-phase project to embed Bridges in the Specialized Dockets Section; the Dispute Resolution Section; the Children, Family and the Courts Section; and the Judicial College.

In the business sector, in addition to Cascade Engineering, Cincinnati Works (CW) used Bridges constructs and achieved an 85% retention rate while placing 700 workers in entry-level jobs in the Cincinnati area. CW was highlighted by the *Harvard Business Review* as one of the most innovative approaches in the nation. West Michigan TEAM (Tri-sector Employment and Advancement Model) has adapted the Cascade Engineering model to serve light manu-facturing and healthcare providers. The State of Michigan reports that, for every 100 employees served, the state saves $1 million. In Vermont the Working Bridges collaborative of employers earned the 2008 Society for Human Resource Management 2008 Pinnacle Award for the services it developed for low-wage, entry-level employees.

Bridges initiatives are catching on in a number of sectors and states; people are beginning to use the word movement when speaking of Bridges.

Oklahoma was the first state to organize and expand Bridges and Getting Ahead at the state level. At latest count there were 19 active sites and eight in the planning phase. The Salvation Army of Oklahoma and Arkansas is providing the services of Deborah Price to coordinate Bridges activities. Certified Bridges trainers and Getting Ahead facilitators meet quarterly to plan the expansion of Bridges, to enhance their skills, and to share best practices.

Many sites are developing Employer Resource Networks (ERNs), which grew out of The Source in Michigan, which in turn grew out of Cascade Engineering. Some ERNs are offering small-dollar loans to help stabilize low-wage workers.

Getting Ahead was used in prisons in Indiana, Louisiana, Colorado, and Ohio, leading to the development of *Getting Ahead While Getting Out,* a book for returning citizens to use prior to their release. Ohio, Oklahoma, and Maryland were the first states to use the reentry book and model.

The Tennessee Department of Human Services is planning to use Bridges and Getting Ahead across the state.

In addition to their own readiness, there are four good reasons why a Bridges Steering Committee (BSC) should step up to help develop the future story for their communities.

First, people in poverty are being hit hardest by the economic meltdown. In"Recession Could Cause Large Increases in Poverty and Push Millions into Deep Poverty,"published November 24, 2008, Sharon Parrott reports that Goldman Sachs projected that unemployment rates will rise to 9% by the fourth quarter of 2009, the number of poor Americans will rise by 7.5% (10.3 million people), and the number of poor children will rise by 2.6% (3.3 million children). The number of children in deep poverty is projected to increase by as much as 2 million.[i] As it turns out, the national unemployment rate already hit 9.5% by July 2009.

What makes this crisis so serious for the poor is that the safety net has huge holes in it through which they will fall. Parrott states: "… [L]ow-income workers who lose their jobs are less likely to qualify for unemployment benefits than higher-income workers, due to eligibility rules in place in many states that deny benefits to individuals who worked part time or did not earn enough during a 'base period' that often excludes workers' most recent employment." In addition, federal and state policies in the 1980s and 1990s have eliminated general assistance programs so that "… about 40 percent of families eligible for cash assistance under the Temporary Assistance for Needy Families (TANF) program will actually receive it." And the unemployed without children will not be eligible for any type of cash assistance.

Second, many people and sectors are not at the table when community development is being considered. Last to be included are those at the bottom of the economic ladder. A Bridges Steering Committee can provide the way to include and engage everyone in problem solving and building a community where everyone can live well.

Third, it's at the community level that the BSC can have the highest impact; this is where we have solid relationships, knowledge of local conditions, access to resources, and influence. By working locally we can help individuals and families in poverty by identifying the barriers to fulfilling their dreams and bringing social capital to bear.

Fourth, BSCs have the ideas, lexicon, tools, and capacity that a community needs.

WHAT BRIDGES STEERING COMMITTEES CAN OFFER THEIR COMMUNITIES

FOUNDATIONAL IDEAS

- The lens of economic class as a way to address poverty

- A common language for poverty and class issues

- A way to address all the causes of poverty: individual choices and circumstances, community conditions, exploitation, and political/economic structures

- An understanding of the impact of income and wealth disparity on individuals and communities

- Accurate mental models of the environments of poverty, middle class, and wealth on which communities can base their plans

- An understanding that people in poverty are problem solvers

- An understanding of the hidden rules of economic class that arise from one's environment

- A way to use the knowledge of hidden rules to develop relationships of mutual respect and to design programs more skillfully

- A shared definition of poverty that is more than an income guideline, one that gives individuals and communities a way to end poverty by building resources

- A way to address race and poverty issues that puts the focus on income and wealth disparity, as well as wealth creation

- An understanding of the importance of having a stable environment

- Identifying four ways to get out of poverty: ownership of one's own future story, a good job, an education that leads to a good paying job, and bridging social capital

- A focus on reducing barriers to getting out of poverty and providing long-term support for people as they make the transition out of poverty

SUPPORTS AND TOOLS FROM AHA! PROCESS, INC.

- Large list of books, workbooks, CDs, DVDs, research manuals, and other products

- Flexible training opportunities

- Trainer Certification to establish a contingent of local trainers to develop critical mass

- Technical support

- Licensed Bridges sites: expand the capacity to deliver high-quality workshops and technical support by region

STRUCTURES AND MODELS

- Bridges Steering Committees

- Engaging all classes, races, sectors, and political persuasions at the decision-making table

- Strategies for change at the individual, organization, community, and policy level

CHAMPIONS

- Early adopters/adapters from several disciplines/sectors that become learning centers—in schools, businesses, workforce development, courts, social services, post-secondary

PARTNERS

- Cascade Engineering

- Cincinnati Works

COMMUNITY OF PRACTICE

- Growing number of Bridges Community sites

- Annual institutes for peer learning and introduction of new ideas

- Websites

- Newsletters

- Webinars

- Taped conference calls

INTRODUCING THE BRIDGES CONTINUUM— A TOOL FOR COMPREHENSIVE PLANNING

People in almost every sector and discipline are attracted to Bridges constructs. It's not long before they come to own the ideas and apply them in their unique ways. That sort of creativity generates energy, feeding the learning of others who seek them out. New ideas and applications are spinning off the core ideas faster than we can track them. The Bridges Continuum is a way to organize the work of a BSC and encourage innovations and new strategies.

THE BRIDGES CONTINUUM
COMPREHENSIVE STRATEGIES FOR BRIDGES STEERING COMMITTEES

	Pre-conception to 6	K–12	Postsecondary	Workforce Prep/Placement
Metrics: Ending Poverty Scorecard	Ready for school Language experience, brain development, cognitive learning structures	Graduation rates GEDs	Retention rates Graduation rates Certifications	Employment rate Apprenticeships Certifications Availability of jobs Mix of jobs
Fallout Costs	Failure to act here means giving up the highest returns on dollars spent on interventions; for birth to 5 the returns can be as high as 15–17%. [i]	Dropouts from the class of 2007 will cost the U.S. nearly $329 billion in lost wages, taxes, and productivity in their lifetimes. [ii]	Loss of income: lifetime earnings of a male with a bachelor's degree in 2004 were 96% higher than a male with a high school diploma. [iii]	Crime imposes costs of as much as $1–2 trillion per year. The savings that can be realized by preventing crime and delinquency among youths are extremely high. [iv]
Family of Strategies Using aha! Process Constructs	*Tucker Signing Strategies* *Reading by Age 5* Getting Ahead with parents Develop an early-childhood champion Bridges Early Childhood Community of Practice	Ruby Payne schools— Framework training *The R Rules* *Collaboration For Kids* Dropout prevention Financial literacy	*Investigations into Economic Class in America* *Understanding and Engaging Under-Resourced College Students* (for faculty and instructors) Achievement Alliance Community of Practice	Cascade Engineering/Quest Cincinnati Works The Source Getting Ahead Future Story Project, IN Bridges Business Community of Practice
Who Takes Responsibility for Change	Families, early-childhood development field	Parents, students, educators, school boards, PTAs, taxpayers	Students, faculty, administrators, boards, communities, benefactors	Employers, employees, government, colleges, chambers of commerce, economic and community developers, workforce development, high schools

[i] Heckman, James J. "Investing in Disadvantaged Young Children is an Economically Efficient Policy." Paper presented at Committee for Economic Development, the Pew Charitable Trusts, PNC Financial Services Group Forum on "Building the Economic Case for Investments in Preschool." New York, January 10, 2006.
[ii] High School Dropouts in America, Alliance for Excellent Education, http://www.all4ed.org/files/GraduationRates_FactSheet.pdf
[iii] Kirsch, Irwin, Braun, Henry, Yamamoto, Kentaro. (January, 2007). "America's Perfect Storm: Three Forces Changing Our Nation's Future." Princeton, NJ: Educational Testing Service.
[iv] Holzer, Harry J. "Workforce Development and the Disadvantaged." The Urban Institute, Brief 7, September 2008. www.urban.org/UploadPDF/411761_workforce_development.PDF

Note. Adapted by Scott Miller (Move the Mountain, Inc.) and Philip DeVol (aha! Process, Inc.).

Prepared by Scott Miller of Move the Mountain, Inc.
and Philip DeVol of aha! Process, Inc.

www.ahaprocess.com
www.movethemountain.org
© 2009 by aha! Process, Inc.
© 2009 Move the Mountain

Job Retention	Self-Sufficient Income	Seniors	Wellness	Community Prosperity
One-year minimum	Self-sufficient wage (Wider Opportunities for Women) 200% poverty guidelines goals met for households Assets established	Poverty rate Access to housing and health care	High resources—all 11 Balanced life Giving back to the community	Environmental sustainability Economic viability where everyone can live well Low rates of poverty and disparity Social Health Indices are positive
$5,505.08 average turnover cost for an $8.00 an hour employee [v]	Children who live in families with an annual income less than $15,000 are 22 times more likely to be abused or neglected than children living in families with an annual income of $30,000 or more. [vi]	Individuals 55 and older accounted for 22% of all personal bankruptcies in 2007, compared with 8% in 1991. Healthcare costs proved to be the top reason for many of these bankruptcies. [vii]	Poor rankings in the OECD (Organization for Economic Co-operation and Development) [viii]	Persistent childhood poverty is estimated to cost our nation $500 billion a year, or about 4% of GDP. [ix] Communities that have lost manufacturing jobs, businesses, and their tax base are not viable economically and socially.
Cascade Engineering/Quest Cincinnati Works The Source Getting Ahead for new employees Working Bridges Employer Workgroup, Vermont Bridges Business Community of Practice	Employer in-house advancement strategies Bridges training Getting Ahead Cascade Engineering/ Quest Cincinnati Works The Source Bridges Business Community of Practice	Wider Opportunities for Women	Comprehensive delivery systems Community Collaboration and Integration (CCI) Bridges to Health Community of Practice *Tactical Communication* Bridges Criminal Justice Community of Practice	Bridges Steering Committees Community Sustainability Grid Systemic change and policy issues sectors Bridges Communities of Practice
Employers, employees, chambers of commerce, economic and community developers, workforce development, human services, government	Policymakers, employers, employees, workforce development, government, human services	Service providers, faith community, government, neighborhood associations, civic groups	Faith community, civic organizations, medical community, law enforcement, neighborhood associations, political parties	Bridges Steering Committees, people and organizations from all other points on the continuum. People from all classes, races, and political persuasions

[v] Compilation of Turnover Studies, SASHA Corporation, http://www.sashacorp.com/turnframe.html
[vi] American Humane, http://www.americanhumane.org/about-us/newsroom/fact-sheets/americas-children.html
[vii] Health Care Costs, Economy Pushing Senior Citizens to Bankruptcy and Poverty in the U.S., Senior Journal.com. http://seniorjournal.com/NEWS/SeniorStats/2008/20080826-USSeniorCitizensInPoverty.htm
[viii] Burd-Sharps, Sarah, et al. (2008) The Measure of America: American Human Development Report 2008-2009. New York, NY: Columbia University Press.
[ix] Center for American Progress, From Poverty to Prosperity: A National Strategy to Cut Poverty in Half, April 2007. www.americanprogress.org/issues/2007/04/pdf/poverty_report.pdf.

KEY ELEMENTS OF THE BRIDGES CONTINUUM

The continuum covers life experiences from cradle to grave. These include the early years at home, going to school, working, and old age. Communities need strategies for people at all stages of life. Along the continuum, BSCs must consider how to alleviate the effects of poverty, how to prevent it, how to help people move out of it, and how to end it.

The Wellness column was added because there's more to life than going to school and work. For a balanced life, all resources must be nurtured: financial, mental, emotional, social, physical, spiritual, relationships/role models, motivation, integrity, and knowledge of hidden rules. Community organizations can do a great deal to help stabilize the life of those in poverty and to help build resources. It's important to note that this continuum is not organized around the structure of federal and state departments and their local entities. In other words, with the exception of K–12 and postsecondary education, there isn't a column for TANF, healthcare, criminal justice, domestic violence, behavioral healthcare, faith-based initiatives, child and adult protection services, and so on. That would be dividing our work in the usual way and would continue to support the "silos" in which we do our work.

The column for Community Prosperity is to remind us that our lives are shaped by the community in which we live. We want to overcome the passive acceptance of things as they are in our locality and motivate ourselves and others to create a place where everyone can live well. The BSC must establish a vision that is greater than the collective missions of the member organizations.

Metrics: A Bridges Steering Committee will need simple and meaningful indicators of success, with the data to be used for quality improvement activities and to assist in deciding what initiatives to support.

Fallout costs: As a nation we have failed to end poverty because our strategies have not been comprehensive. We pay the cost when we don't address poverty at every stage of life. We must address poverty from both the head and the heart; the costs are not only financial but human. Too much poverty brings down individuals, families, and communities.

Strategies: This column names the initiatives, products, trainings, partners, and champions that make it possible for a Bridges Community to do its work. Collectively we have the tools, as well as the necessary constructs. This column also acknowledges that we need more learning, more champions, and more partners.

Responsibility: In this column we make the point that responsibility to end poverty and to build prosperous communities lies with everyone—individuals, families, organizations, businesses, policymakers, funders, and the BSCs.

USES AND VALUE OF THE BRIDGES CONTINUUM

System thinkers

- The Bridges Continuum attracts people from all sectors.

- It illustrates the big picture—strategies for the entire life cycle and the need for individual, organizational, and community change.

- It makes the argument that we can't afford poverty; the costs of poverty are too high and threaten the viability of the entire community.

- It illustrates that aha! Process and its partners have the necessary constructs and tools needed to end poverty.

Investors/funders

- It attracts funders; they can see where their investments fit in the larger picture.

- It will leverage funds from others who see the long-term value of high-impact strategies.

Community partners

- It attracts new partners; every sector and organization can identify where it fits on the continuum and how its work is related to the work of others.

- It will help develop new partnerships between private and public sectors.

- It encourages all member organizations on the BSC to apply these tools in their own setting.

- It shows the role that champions play and encourages the development of champions in all disciplines and sectors.

Strategies and efficiencies

- It will help develop innovative, high-impact strategies.

- It illustrates the interconnectedness of the sectors and points to the potential for cost-effective collaborations.

- It defines the metrics to guide evaluations and quality-improvement activities.

- It encourages cost-effectiveness.

Principles

- It illustrates a paradigm shift; no longer is it just the job of the individual to get out of poverty or for social services to end poverty; now every sector has a role to play.

- It shows that addressing poverty isn't just about jobs, education, or social capital; it's all of those things and fostering a well-rounded, balanced life.

WAYS THAT BRIDGES STEERING COMMITTEES CAN USE THE CONTINUUM

First, identify the organizations that are doing work along the continuum. Ideally, those organizations would be using Bridges constructs in the design and delivery of their programs. For example, take the organizations with early childhood development programs, which would fit in the Birth to 6 column. The questions to them would be: How successful are you at attracting and involving people in poverty? Do your products and approaches work best with middle-class parents and children? Have they been tailored to serve families in poverty? How would the organization use the continuum and all of the following tools to improve outcomes with clients from poverty?

The continuum is one of two Bridges tools that help a community do comprehensive work. The first to be introduced to a Bridges Community is the Community Sustainability Grid. It was designed to address all causes of poverty and to help planners avoid the tendency to either blame the individual or blame the system. Starting with the familiar grid below, add the new tool as a way of deepening the strategies and applications.

COMMUNITY SUSTAINABILITY GRID				
	Individual Choices and Circumstances	Community: Human and Social Capital	Exploitation	Political/ Economic Structures
Individual action				
Organizational action				
Community action				
Policy action				

Now bring the two tools together: The column headings are from the Community Sustainability Grid; the rows are from the Bridges Continuum.

	Individual	Community: Human and Social Capital	Exploitation	Political/ Economic Structures
Birth to 6				
K–12				
Post-secondary				
Workforce prep/placement				
Retention				
Self-sufficient wage				
Senior				
Wellness				
Community prosperity				

Taking the row Workforce prep/placement, let's "drill down" to see how the two tables can help us deepen our work.

Workforce Prep/Placement and Individual Choices and Circumstances

Bridges constructs to consider here are: motivation and responsibilities of the individual, accountability of the individual to oneself and others, the relationship of the people involved in terms of language and mutual respect, commitment to the potential employer, and the access the individual has to Bridges information.

Example: At Cincinnati Works (CW), which places 700 people a year in worksites with a retention rate of 85%, preparation is done in just under 40 hours. Participation at CW is voluntary; once a person joins, that person becomes a lifelong member of CW. The member makes an "I'll call before I quit" promise to both CW and the employer. CW will be monitoring and supporting the member at the workplace and will make every effort to remove barriers that may interfere with the member's regular attendance.

In other settings employees are offered Getting Ahead, a group learning experience that introduces them to Bridges constructs. One value of Getting Ahead is that it helps employees identify their future stories and articulate their own motivation.

Workforce Prep/Placement and Community

Things to consider are the availability of jobs, the willingness of employers to hire people from poverty, and strategies for removing barriers that interfere with regular work participation.

Example: The St. Joseph County Bridges Out of Poverty Initiative in South Bend, Indiana, asked 16 employers to become members of the Future Story Project (FSP) and hire Getting Ahead graduates; eight agreed to become involved in the FSP. The FSP is a public/private partnership to remove barriers to employment and to improve retention rates.

Workforce Prep/Placement and Exploitation

Things to consider are offering jobs with a line of sight to better-paying jobs, benefits, and employee supports that help employees avoid predatory lending outlets.

Example: In Vermont, "Working Bridges," a public/private partnership, has implemented an emergency loan and savings program for employees in partnership with North Country Federal Credit Union; has piloted a worksite resource coordinator model in three companies to aid employees in finding help with housing, childcare, transportation, economic assistance, and other resources without having to leave work; and has begun discussions about how to develop effective health and wellness strategies for economically diverse workforces.

Workforce Prep/Placement and Political/Economic Structures

Things to consider are entry-level wages, benefits, health coverage, accountability systems, and educational opportunities.

Examples: At Cincinnati Works, members are placed with employers whose beginning wage is no less than $8.50 an hour. The goal is to get all CW members to an income that is 200% of the poverty guideline.

Since the Bucks County, Pennsylvania, Economic Self-Sufficiency Program was established in 1997, a total of 182 participants have graduated and eliminated the need for government TANF subsidies; secured employment that pays a family-sustaining wage; established a balanced household budget and bank account; and attained family health insurance, safe and affordable housing, and safe and reliable transportation. Fifty graduates are homeowners, and every dollar invested in the program saves the community at least four dollars in government subsidies, such as TANF, Food Stamps, and subsidized housing.

IN BRIDGES COMMUNITIES, SERVICES AND PROGRAMS ARE DESIGNED TO MEET ONE OR MORE OF THESE FOUR PURPOSES:

To alleviate the effects of poverty: Food stamps, food pantries, shelters for the homeless, cash assistance, insurance for children, healthcare are all elements of the safety net provided to people in poverty. Government takes the lead, with faith-based groups and non-governmental organizations filling in the gaps. In addition, there are programs for those who suffer from child abuse, domestic violence, addiction, mental illness, health issues, and disabilities. Rich nations are distinguished from poor nations by the safety net they provide for the vulnerable members of their society. States and cities that cannot balance their budgets and whose tax base has eroded are unraveling the safety net by "defunding" programs.

To prevent poverty: Early-childhood development programs, education, after-school activities, sports programs, and prevention programming of all sorts play a large role in developing opportunities for young people. Everyone in the prevention field knows that, for every dollar spent on prevention, society saves $7 on intervention and treatment costs. This is most crucial in preventing drug addiction, health problems, and criminal behavior. States, cities, and organizations that triage services in hard economic times cut prevention first. Ironically, this is exactly what people do when they don't have enough money.

To support transition out of poverty: Workforce development, Section 8 housing, Habitat for Humanity, probation services, clothing for the job, childcare, insurance, and soft-skill training are public and private programs conceived to provide support. Given a chance to reflect on and examine their situation in poverty, most people have a vision or goal of getting out of poverty. And the message from the dominant culture is that everyone should be self-sufficient and a contributing member of society, i.e., everyone should pay their share of taxes. So why is it so hard for people to get out of poverty?

Unfortunately, many public programs have cliff effects—the loss of benefits as income increases. In Oklahoma, for example, children are eligible for Medicaid up to 185% of the federal poverty guideline. This is an all-or-nothing benefit, so the plunge into the pool of the uninsured can result from a small increase in income.[ii] In addition, these private and public programs are rarely coordinated. People in poverty spend a great deal of time doing "agency time," moving from agency to agency, filling out forms and providing the same information again and again—and being subject to the plans developed at each site.

To create communities where everyone can live well:
Many people think of the period between 1947 and 1979 as the golden age of the middle class. Real family income growth went up for everyone: 116% for the poorest 20% of people and 99% for the wealthiest. The second, third, and fourth quintiles saw increases of 100%, 111%, and 114%, respectively. All boats floated higher during that period.

Since then, the divide between the rich and poor has been growing dramatically. Middle-class incomes have flatlined since the late '70s, and middle-class jobs are becoming increasingly less stable. The working class are slipping into situational poverty; many low-wage workers are now relying on food stamps. In these very hard times, we in Bridges Communities are working to see people get out of poverty.

Community by community, Bridges is making a difference as we reduce barriers, open up opportunities, and address all the causes of poverty. The Bridges movement must begin to address policies at the county, state, and federal levels.

Defining these purposes can help a Bridges Steering Committee think about where to put its energy and resources. Here are some questions to consider:

- Most programs have an obvious purpose. What is the purpose of each BSC initiative?

- Member organizations are providing services to people in poverty. What is the purpose of each of those programs? Have those programs been redesigned, and are they using Bridges constructs?

- Which purpose typically gets the most funding?

- When do programs designed to alleviate the effects of poverty inadvertently foster dependency?

- What safety nets are necessary for the members of our community who cannot hope to survive without assistance?

- How can programs that alleviate the effects of poverty still encourage and support the dreams of those who suffer the most severe disabilities and problems?

- Given that poverty drives people into the "tyranny of the moment," how can prevention programs be fine-tuned to effectively engage and serve people in poverty?

- How should funding be shared and allocated among alleviation, prevention, transition, and elimination?

- How can programs be designed to serve more than one purpose?

OVERCOMING THE BARRIERS TO CHANGE AT THE ORGANIZATIONAL AND COMMUNITY LEVELS

An informal review of Bridges Communities shows that it's harder (and takes longer) to apply Bridges constructs at the organizational level than it is to add such programs as Getting Ahead. The champions that have applied Bridges effectively—Cascade Engineering, Cincinnati Works, courts, etc.—tend to be organizations where leaders can make changes happen. They are speedboats that can turn on a dime compared with the ocean liners that are driven by federal and state legislation or by complicated self-imposed structures, such as those found in the healthcare field. It takes a long time to turn an ocean liner. In fact, Bridges Communities can achieve collaborative initiatives, or they can challenge predatory lending practices more readily than some of the member organizations can apply Bridges in their own shops.

Unfortunately, in order to effectively address poverty, most organizations will have to change the way they do business. BSC members might ask themselves ...

Knowing the key concepts of Bridges and Getting Ahead:

- Do we need to change our mission, theory of change, program designs, policies, or procedures to better serve people in poverty—and to contribute to a high-impact Bridges initiative?

- If so, who within our own organization is needed to make the changes happen?

- Who from outside the organization might help make the changes?

- Where does our work fit on the Bridges Continuum? Where else can it fit?

- Where does it fit on the Community Sustainability Grid? Is our focus on one or two causes of poverty? Does it need to be expanded?

- Does our organization focus on alleviating, preventing, assisting with transition, or eliminating poverty? Or does it address a combination of one or more of these? Does our focus need to be expanded?

Member organizations of the Bridges Community have the creativity and organizational skills to answer these questions, decide what must be done, and do it. Nonetheless—and in the interest of making it easier—here are some groups and people who can help.

The Bridges Community of Practice: This term applies to all communities that have applied Bridges concepts. As organizations and communities take ownership of Bridges, they become learning centers for others. At aha! Process we attempt to bring the community together via webinars, phone conferences, annual Bridges institutes, and websites to share knowledge, strategies, and tools (see www.bridgesoutofpoverty.com). You're encouraged to take advantage of this learning community.

SupplyCore, Inc. and Simon Solutions, Inc. are two partners that provide Bridges Steering Committees and Bridges organizations with evaluation tools for Getting Ahead graduates and tools for client-centered case-treatment planning and resource management. SupplyCore offers MPOWR, and Simon Solutions offers Charity-Tracker Plus.

Organizations using Bridges and Getting Ahead can use the solutions offered by either of the partners to evaluate Getting Ahead graduates and to provide client-centered case planning.

Communities that form a Bridges Steering Committee can build a powerful collaborative when all the Bridges organizations agree to use the same tool. There are communities where as many as 40 organizations are using either MPOWR or CharityTracker. In those communities it is possible for individual sites and the collaborative to generate reports for themselves, the community, and funders.

Bridges consulting and training: aha! Process has Bridges consultants available to assist with the redesign of your programs. They bring with them a wealth of knowledge rooted in research and practical experience (see www.bridgesoutofpoverty.com).

There are many consultants who specialize in organizational change. If the goal is to embed Bridges constructs in the organization, it's imperative that the consultants are fully conversant with Bridges concepts.

There is one particular barrier to change that must be mentioned. For individuals and families in poverty, it's both ironic and sad that one of the greatest barriers to people getting out of poverty are the very organizations that make it their mission to improve the lives of those who are in poverty. Allow me to elaborate.

The main culprit is the organizational silo. This somewhat overused metaphor still works to describe how several silos in one city or county, all serving people in poverty, can all do good work within their own discipline or department but still fail to get people out of poverty. In fact, in big organizations it's possible to have silos inside silos—various departments that operate independently of each other and sometimes (from the client's point of view) at cross-purposes. There's an analogy here with the impact on people of color of many predominantly white power structures and systems. The individuals in those systems almost never are intentionally racist in how they operate, but a cumulative impact of those structures is still felt by many people of color. Similar "intent vs. impact" analysis applies to well-intentioned social workers who, nonetheless, work in silos, often resulting in a negative impact on people in poverty as little coordination happens between and among most agencies—and people in poverty are run through virtually the same "wringer" time after time.

The problem with silos is that administrators get really good at achieving outcomes that at the very least justify continued funding. An agency might be good at helping people get sober, but that doesn't mean other aspects of the person's life have improved. He or she might still be living in a very stressful and unstable environment, still in poverty. The client's life is experienced not in compartments or by departments, but as an interconnected whole.

Silos aren't going away; they are too deeply embedded in educational, governmental, and funding systems. So communities must learn to operate above the silos. BSC members must leave their silo mentality at the door when they come together to plan.

To emphasize the importance of this, consider these two points:

First, there is the problem of the implied promise. This occurs when people in poverty enter the silos for help. The implied promise is, "By coming here, things will be better for you." From the point of view of someone in poverty, this promise is broken—again and again— at the three to nine agencies they go to in the course of a year.[iii] The promise is broken because the person in poverty doesn't live in our silos; they live a whole life. Our silos can offer addictions recovery in one, education in another, safety in yet another, but stability and getting out of poverty are rarely measurable outcomes for any one silo. There is no federal or state department or board of directors that holds the silos accountable for helping people out of poverty. So the promise that "by coming here, things will be better" is broken. It's no wonder that people in poverty come to distrust our institutions.

Second, those of us who operate silos get stuck—just as stuck in our way of doing business as people in poverty get stuck in poverty. Not only do we become fixed in the way we see our clients and the way we treat them, but we become fixed in the way we treat our employees. Isn't it ironic that many nonprofits that serve people in poverty pay poverty wages? How can we expect our clients to get out of poverty if our employees can't? There is dignity in work, but work without hope of advancement and economic stability is asking too much and providing too little.

The way out for both people in poverty and the organizations that serve them is to develop a new future story. We do this by recognizing that the way we are living now is not the way we want to live. We analyze the way things are, we learn new things, we dream up a new future, and we pursue it. It's all about the future story.

WHOLE SYSTEM PLANNING— WORKING ABOVE THE SILOS

There is a city in Brazil that stands as a shining example of whole system planning. I had first read about Curitiba in Paul Hawken's book *Natural Capitalism* and mentioned it during a workshop attended by Hope Taft, the First Lady of Ohio at that time. We talked about our shared interest in Curitiba, not knowing an Ohio Business Mission to South America had already been planned. Hope invited me to join the business mission so, in January 2001, we went to Curitiba with the business mission to see for ourselves how a Third World city the size of Houston could achieve amazing results in education, housing, transportation, and air quality. Curitiba has the best air quality of any city its size in the world, a home ownership rate of 75%, and a high school graduation rate of 85%.

Jaime Lerner, first elected mayor of Curitiba in 1971, was the principal driving force behind the changes in Curitiba. By 2001 he had served several terms as mayor and was now the governor of the state of Parna, in which Curitiba is located. He's an architect, engineer, and urban planner. He used interdisciplinary charrettes, an architect's planning and design process, to bring together everyone connected with an initiative. He then had them work in small groups before consolidating all the ideas. Hope Taft and I met people who were involved in various projects; in every case we met people from different academic backgrounds and disciplines. The budget and plan were not controlled or driven by any particular department but by teams of people who were committed to a set of higher principles and goals.

This is whole system planning. Hawken said it was done "… by implementing hundreds of multipurpose, cheap, fast, simple, home-grown, people-centered initiatives harnessing market mechanisms, common sense, and local skills. It has flourished by treating all its citizens—most of all its children—not as its burden but as its most precious resource, creators of its future. It has succeeded not by central planning but by combining farsighted and pragmatic leadership with an integrated design process, strong public and business participation, and a widely shared public vision that transcends partisanship."[iv]

Curitiba has clean air because of its bus system, which carries three-fourths of the city's commuters. I had to ride the bus to see how quickly passengers could enter and exit the buses by using a flip-down "drawbridge" at every door of the buses. Riders would use the drawbridge to exit, not to the ground, but on to a station platform above the sidewalk. The stations were huge, Plexiglas-type tubes that protected riders from the weather and allowed the flow of riders to reach street level quickly. The system carries 20,000 passengers an hour. The bus driver controls the traffic lights so it tends to speed things up. The bus system takes workers to the Western companies that are attracted to Curitiba. It is self-financed by fares and the flat-rate, unlimited-transfer fares mean that the poor are able to use the system. The bus runs on ethanol.

The poor get generous food tickets by doing the city's recycling. Recycling containers are found at every corner, and city planners tear down and reuse materials from old buildings. In 2001 old telephone poles were reused to build a sound stage for music events at the old stone quarry. It is the most recycling-friendly city I have ever seen.

The poor can get into homeownership with sweat equity and by taking classes in fiscal literacy. Most of their homes eight years ago were 400 square feet with a small, walled-in yard. There were 200 daycare centers, free to the poor, that stayed open 14 hours a day and served four meals.

Municipal services are streamlined to save time. Wrote Hawken:"…
[A] sick mother can schedule a clinic or specialist appointment, day
care, and any other required support with a single phone call."[v] The
city essentially serves as a huge employee assistance program for
working people and the companies that employ them. Lerner asked
only that Western light-manufacturing firms pay a decent wage.

Instead of trying to control flooding with canals and dams, they
created wetlands so that when the waters rise the only effect is that
the ducks float a meter higher. In the dry season, the wetlands are
grazed by sheep to avoid the use of lawnmowers.

We visited the "24-hour street" that is open to young people who
need a safe place to go. The police are there to protect young people,
not to take them into custody. On the 24-hour street young people
find inexpensive food and Internet cafés.

Hope and I visited a Lighthouse of Knowledge, a 50-foot-tall, light-
house-shaped library holding a selection of books and offering
Internet access to students. Poor students can receive and keep
school books in exchange for recyclable refuse. At night a policeman
stands atop the lighthouse to protect the community. The Curitiba
goal is to have a Lighthouse of Knowledge within walking distance
of every child's home.

These achievements were the result of the mindset of the planners
and their way of doing business. Lerner's mindset toward people in
poverty is expressed this way: "If people feel respected, they will
assume responsibility to help solve other problems."[vi]

Analyzing the Curitiba story gives us a way to look at our own work,
first by examining our mindset regarding our work in the community,
then looking at models and structures, and finally looking at tools.

The mindset and principles underlying the work in Curitiba and
Bridges Communities is similar:

- People in poverty are involved as problem solvers, all disciplines and sectors are engaged, there is a shared focus on a particular issue, solutions are local, partnerships are formed between different sectors, and ownership is high. In Curitiba and in Bridges Communities the work is based on relationships of mutual respect. Those who are familiar with *Getting Ahead in a Just-Gettin'-By World,* written in 2003, will recognize just how much Curitiba influenced the workbook.

- Every BSC, every community, has a different history, approach, and structure—and that's how it should be. But we can share a mindset and a world view, and we can share models, organizational structures, and tools that help us get our work done.

Curitiba is an inspiring example of what happens when a community operates above the silos, where the silo mindset is left at the door during meetings, and where there's an intention to help families achieve a stable environment and get out of poverty.

Lerner was quite conscious of outcomes and metrics; he had to be as he was working with a Third World budget. The unit cost he used to bring meaning to a project is the cost of asphalting a kilometer of street. For example, a Lighthouse of Knowledge costs the equivalent of 0.2 kilometers of asphalt.

What unit cost could we use? A quick search of the Internet reveals that in the U.S. one mile of highway construction costs about $1 million. Another possible unit cost could be the annual expense to house a drug offender in prison, which is approximately $24,000. BSCs might want to establish local unit costs to illustrate the value of their initiatives.

METRICS THAT REALLY MATTER

Unit costs are only one metric or measure that a community will need to establish. The saying"You can't fix what you don't measure" applies here. To expand on the topic of metrics that were touched on in the Bridges Continuum will help prepare BSCs for the work that lies ahead.

Bridges sites are dedicated to helping families get out of poverty by stabilizing their world and building resources. This has been made harder by the erosion of wealth-creating mechanisms that once helped create a stable middle class. Now the middle class in the U.S. is shrinking, and more people are slipping into poverty. It's in this difficult environment that Bridges is working to help people make the transition out of poverty.

Put simply, poverty for an individual or family is defined as instability in daily life, being afraid for today and the future. A lack of resources forces people into spending lots of time solving the same problems over and over again.

Middle class is defined as having stability in daily life. People in middle class have today covered, but they're afraid about the future. Having healthcare insurance and a AAA card can smooth out problems of the day, but pensions or 401(k)s may not be secure.

Wealth is defined as having stability today and in the future. For those in wealth, fear is about the loss of assets and connections, as well as the ability to maintain a particular lifestyle.

METRICS FOR THE INDIVIDUAL OR FAMILY

What are the metrics that really matter for an individual in his or her daily life? What does it take to have economic stability? In Getting Ahead groups the investigators explore the following metrics:

Debt-to-income (DTI) ratio: In Module 2 of Getting Ahead the investigators discover the importance of their DTI ratio. A debt load of over 37% is a sign of trouble[vii] as Edmund L. Andrews, an *economics* reporter for the *New York Times*, discovered when he lost track of this basic measure. On the strength of his credit rating he bought a home he couldn't afford and—despite the help of (or perhaps because of) a loan officer of a mortgage corporation—Andrews plunged into a series of go-go mortgages, liar's loans, piggyback loans, and a no-ratio mortgage that led to foreclosure.[viii]

Percentage of income that goes to housing: In Module 2 of Getting Ahead, investigators discovered that 30% is the metric that matters. Those who adhered to this metric would have avoided foreclosures when the mortgage industry imploded.

Saving accounts and building assets: Income changes on a dime with the jobs that come and go. Wealth or assets—such as property, savings, investments, and businesses—are built up over time and passed on to the next generation. Putting part of each paycheck into a savings account before you pay your bills is the first step in building stability. By paying yourself first you can build a rainy-day fund for when the car breaks down or you need to move. And, if all goes well, it can become a down payment when buying a house.

Interest rates and fees on loans and credit cards: In Module 4 of Getting Ahead, investigators discovered that unsuspecting, desperate, and avaricious people were duped into loans where interest rates and fees were designed to trap borrowers in constant debt. In that climate, according to Getting Ahead investigators, people who did pay off the balance of their credit card debt every month were called "deadbeats" by the industry.

Wages: In Module 2 of Getting Ahead, the group explores the meaning and impact of wages on one's stability. The *minimum wage* is not a meaningful metric, as it has never been enough to lift a family out of poverty. The living wage, however, is a potential metric. By most definitions it is calculated to provide a family enough to meet the minimum standard of living for their locale. A *self-sufficient wage*, as proposed by Wider Opportunities for Women, is the metric that matters for families. It calculates how much money is needed to meet basic needs without subsidies of any kind. It accounts for the costs of living that vary by family size and composition, as well as location.

Health insurance: Stress-related illnesses are directly correlated with poverty.[ix] Health insurance is an absolute necessity. Medical problems can lead to job loss and medical debt. People with medical problems find it hard to get work and insurance. Most U.S. insurance companies put a great deal of effort into keeping high-risk people out of the pool of those who are covered. These conditions lead to what is known as the death spiral, not to mention a shortened life.[x]

Resources: In modules 6 and 8 Getting Ahead investigators explore and assess their own resources. They are: financial, emotional, mental, spiritual, physical, language, motivation, integrity, support systems, relationships/role models, and knowledge of the hidden rules of class. The higher the 11 resources, the higher the quality of life.

Ultimately the metric that matters the most is: Did life become more stable?

METRICS FOR THE CITY OR COUNTY

What are the metrics that really matter for a city or county? What does it take to have a stable community? The definition of poverty, middle class, and wealthy communities is the same as it is for individuals. Poverty for a city or county is defined as instability in daily life, with elected officials being afraid for today and the future. The mayors, city council members, and county commissioners are driven by lost tax revenue to focus on survival issues. Services are cut, crime increases, jobs disappear, housing stock lies empty, and the quality of life drops. Community leaders tend to be focused on stamping out fires, not on innovation and wealth creation. Their fear for the future is that they won't be able to generate the revenue to recoup the quality of life their community once enjoyed. The tyranny of the moment that deprives individuals in poverty of their future orientation is a phenomenon that also applies to organizations. In the book

The Art of the Long View: Planning for the Future in an Uncertain World, business writer Peter Schwartz notes, "Introducing new perspectives at the moment of decision, when an organization is confronted with the need to act, will inevitably be inadequate. The need to act overwhelms any willingness people have to learn."[xi] Elected leaders of middle-class cities or counties enjoy economic stability in the present, but they fear what the future might hold. Wealthy cities or counties are stable in the present; officials have every expectation of a stable future as well.

It's impossible to talk about helping people make the transition out of poverty, or move out of an unstable environment, without talking about how wealth is created. What wealth-creating mechanisms are in place? How does the community create and support a middle-class lifestyle? In other words, how do we help families create a stable environment?

In the U.S. we used to create wealth by manufacturing steel, cars, airplanes, and washing machines. Then we created wealth with high-tech products: computers and software. Recently we created wealth by flipping houses and designing complicated financial instruments. What will be the next wealth-creating mechanisms? Certainly not the service sector where we repair cars, service airplanes, and ostensibly make a living doing other people's laundry.

The World Development Report 2006, "Equity and Development," identified **four metrics for communities** that can bring prosperity to their families. The study showed that the best economic growth came not from a focus on economic development but from focusing on economic development and *equity*.[xii] Equity is defined as:

A fair shot at a well-paying job. Consider the ongoing and current downward pressure on wages that U.S. workers are facing. Globalization has worked positively to narrow the gap in income and wealth between the poorer nations of the world and the wealthier ones. Unfortunately, globalization also has increased the gap between the rich and poor in the U.S. The downward pressure on wages comes from putting some (though not all) workers in competition with workers in poor nations, thus the loss of well-paying manufacturing jobs, along with some service-sector jobs. Too, the breakup and decline of unions has eroded the number of good jobs. The economic downturn that began in 2008 brought down more wages. Many pilots, automakers, civil service workers, and teachers have been forced to take lower wages. Unfortunately, in poverty communities, the best way to get out of poverty is to get out of town. Detroit and Youngstown are half the size they used to be because people had to move to find well-paying jobs. Metrics to capture the economic health of the city or county include:

- Businesses and jobs that pay well in manufacturing

- Businesses and jobs that pay well in green manufacturing and services

- Businesses and jobs that pay well in new technologies

- Entrepreneurship and small-business development with jobs that pay well

- A workforce with the skills to meet the needs of the employers

- A mix of jobs and wages in the city or county

A fair shot at a good education. What are the metrics beyond the usual, and important, graduation rates and performance standards? Does it matter that music, the arts, and sports are dropped from school activities? Does the public education funding mechanism provide high-quality education to every child? Two metrics that really matter, which don't get enough attention or community support, are:

- Cognitive development in the first six years of life. Recent studies have established the importance of brain and cognitive development in the first six years of life, and yet funding for early-childhood development lags far behind the research.[xiii]

- Fiscal education by qualified and trustworthy sources throughout the span of life. Basic fiscal literacy about budgeting, saving, and investing can be introduced and reinforced as the financial situation of society and the individual change. The economy is complex and fast-moving. The financial products are ever-changing, so it's hard for anyone to keep up. Individual needs also change—when one becomes a wage earner, when credit cards become available, when buying one's first house, when retiring. In a study conducted by Roper Starch Worldwide, 70% of Americans reported that they learned to manage their finances on their own![xiv] Learning by trial and error tends not to be a good idea; the payday lender and (sometimes) the banker are not your friends. For that matter, learning from friends who aren't experts (54% of us) isn't smart either. Where we go to learn is crucial. Ideally, we would all have financial advisers, but few of us can afford that. So having experts available at proven, nonprofit organizations is necessary.

A fair shot at good healthcare. A clinical research study published by the *American Journal of Medicine* found that 62% of all bankruptcies in 2007 had a medical cause, up from 8% in 1981.[xv] Too many people in the community are at risk of being undone by medical problems. Metrics to capture the quality of healthcare include:

- Healthcare for everyone that isn't tied to employment

- The percentage of the population that is uninsured

- Indicators of health presented by race, gender, disability, age, and economic class

A fair shot at fair credit. The financial/mortgage/credit fiasco that erupted in the fall of 2008 points to the failure of our society in a particular metric. Metrics that matter are:

- The interest and fees charged by banks, the mortgage industry, and credit card companies

- The activities of banks in regard to the Community Reinvestment Act requirements

- The number of payday lenders, cash-advance outlets, and other lenders that market their products to people in distress in the city and county—and the annual average interest rates that they impose on people seeking loans

- The number of alternative products and outlets that offer fair credit

And then, as noted a couple of pages ago, there are the metrics that describe the financial and political health of a city or county. As we know cities and counties can be trapped in the tyranny of the moment, just as individuals can. When the income dries up and things begin to break down, the focus turns to survival, and the quality of life begins to suffer. The metrics that matter are:

A tax base sufficient to maintain high-quality services, infrastructure, and future community development. In *The Tyranny of Dead Ideas* Matt Miller identifies six dead ideas, including "taxes hurt the economy (and they're always too high)." Miller predicts that the unwritten law that the American people will not tolerate higher taxes is "… about to collide with the real iron law of mathematics." Few leaders have the courage to say it out loud, but experts understand that taxes are going to have to go up.[xvi]

Bridging social capital that brings people together across class and racial lines to solve problems. Robert Putnam, author of *Bowling Alone,* argues that success in life is more strongly associated with one's connections than one's education.[xvii] Relationships can be developed more quickly than an education, job skills, and advancement. The metrics that matter are:

- People of all economic classes, races, sectors, and political persuasion are actively engaged in solving the problem of poverty in the community.
- Local Bridges Communities are active in Bridges collaboratives at the state, national, and international levels.

A social health index that measures the quality of life. The U.S. is the only wealthy nation that doesn't have a social health index. This set of metrics helps communities to plan, budget, develop policies and programs, and be accountable to the community. The index is also a tool that can be used by grant writers looking for data, elected officials when analyzing the impact of pending legislation, media when looking for the context behind stories, students when doing research, and citizens who want to have accurate data to hold communities and the state accountable for the quality of life.[xviii]

■ ■ ■ ■

Jennifer Brunner, my friend and former Ohio secretary of state, urged me to video interview Phil DeVol, co-author of Bridges Out of Poverty and related series. I did, and the interview stuck with me. It just kept rolling around in my head. I began to talk up the interview to folks on my own time, in addition to my role as senior fellow with The Center for Community Solutions.

One of the people I mentioned it to was Ohio State Rep. Tim Derickson. He saw the video, had the same response, and couldn't get the concepts out of his head.

What you find in this 10-minute video is that the Ohio House of Representatives, my old chamber, formed a committee (chaired by Rep. Derickson) that is completely refocusing how we look at poverty, workforce, mental health, drug addiction, and related issues. It is heavily informed by the Bridges books.

Now the Ohio General Assembly has decided to put its money where its mouth is, and is pumping $11.5 million dollars to expand Bridges-type models and create new ones. This is called the Healthier Buckeye program, and is related to Ohio Gov. John Kasich's administration's concern about the need for a long-term case management program.

The Healthier Buckeye program will utilize strong data gathering and analysis. But most importantly, the program represents a collaborative effort between state and private organizations to create a long-term relationship built on respect, and to invite current welfare recipients to understand how they arrived at this point in their lives, what can be done to change their lives, and the skills needed for that goal.

–**Gene Krebs**
Senior fellow at The Center for Community Solutions, Ohio

12 THINKING TOOLS FOR
BRIDGES OUT OF POVERTY INITIATIVES

Published in 2014 www.ahaprocess.com

THEORY AND PRACTICE IN A BRIDGES INITIATIVE

Bridges Out of Poverty workshops are known for changing the way people think about poverty and economic class. People have "aha" moments that deepen into insights that are so powerful that there is no going back to their old way of thinking. These in turn deepen into paradigm shifts that alter every aspect of their work on poverty. It is not the purpose of this paper to reiterate the basic content of Bridges but to distinguish between theory and practice in Bridges work. The practices may be varied and complex but the theory must bring clarity to our work.

THE THEORY

When individuals are under-resourced to the extent that they spend most of their time and energy trying to keep their heads above water, their daily living experience becomes dominated by the tyranny of the moment. Rather than spending time and energy building resources for a better future, their time and energy go toward trying to stabilize their unstable world, and they end up staying stuck in a life of poverty.

When institutions and communities are under-resourced to the extent that they spend too much time and energy trying to keep their heads above water, they behave in very similar ways to under-resourced individuals: They spend their time solving concrete problems using strategies that originate from the same mindset that created the problems.

The solution for individuals, institutions, and communities is to build stability and resources.

THE PRACTICE

Bridges initiatives have a common language about poverty and matters of economic class. Bridges initiatives use the following 12 thinking tools to build stability and resources at four levels: individual, institutional, community, and policy. The goal of Bridges initiatives is to prevent poverty, alleviate suffering, aid those who are making the transition out of poverty, and create communities where everyone can live well.

Anyone familiar with Bridges will be aware of most of the following mental models. Mental models are used to help make abstract ideas more concrete and to help us remember ideas by representing them with visual images. Mental models help us learn quickly, remember longer, and apply the concepts in deeper ways. Thus the term thinking tools.

Mental models tend to provide our first "aha" moment and new insights that attract us to Bridges. For some people, attraction moves quickly to action. Early adapters have generated a number of programs and approaches that have become foundational to the Bridges movement. But poverty is a complex problem that demands a comprehensive approach. And therein lies the challenge. Poverty is not resolved with a single program or even set of programs, because there are so many variables. Bridges is not a program. It is a set of constructs that can be applied in many settings and in many ways.

The ensuing thinking tools can help individuals, organizations, and communities create, embed, and expand solutions.

The pattern for explaining these 12 thinking tools has these six elements:

- A problem statement describing how things are now

- A mental model representing the thinking tool

- The context in which the tool is applied—a description of how it fits into Bridges work

- Core ideas of the thinking tool

- Ways to use the tool

- Information on where to learn more

TABLE OF CONTENTS: 12 THINKING TOOLS

1. TRIPLE LENS

HOW THINGS ARE NOW

Individuals learn about poverty through personal experience, stories in the news, reading, and general debate—but rarely through an intention to fully understand this complex problem. Without a structure for processing the complexities of poverty, without a way to organize our thinking, our responses to poverty will continue to be ineffective.

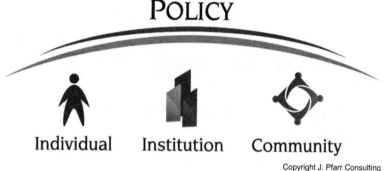

POLICY

Individual   Institution   Community

Copyright J. Pfarr Consulting

A woman in poverty saw a sign on a caseworker's door that read, "Your failure to plan does not constitute an emergency for me." The triple lens has us first analyze the dynamics between the client and caseworker, helping to explore and decode class interactions from both sides of the desk. It would deepen the understanding by analyzing the driving forces of the institution and the role of the institution in the community.

By using the triple lens, we develop new ideas, discover how to apply new concepts, and make necessary changes. This tool helps us do thorough work.

As for clients who are late, it's possible that they might need to make some changes, but this tool reminds us that they don't need to change any more than those who are in the institutions and community.

CONTEXT

The triple lens is a structure by which poverty can be assessed and processed thoroughly. Looking at poverty through a single lens—be it individual, organizational, or community—will not provide the depth of understanding that comes from viewing poverty through all three lenses.

CORE IDEAS

Poverty elicits strong opinions; it's easy to take sides or to blame the other person or institution. This thinking tool helps replace judgments with understanding. The first place that conflicts usually occur is the interaction between people in poverty and people in institutions, such as caseworkers, supervisors, and healthcare workers.

HOW TO USE THE TOOL

- Use the triple lens to deepen understanding of the core elements of a Bridges workshop: the mental models of class, the causes of poverty, hidden rules, resources, and language.

- When embedding the concepts in our organization or designing a new community program, the question becomes: "What would we learn by applying the triple lens?"

LEARN MORE

Read *Tactical Communication: Mastering effective interactions with citizens from diverse economic backgrounds*, Jodi R. Pfarr, 2013.

2. MENTAL MODELS OF ECONOMIC CLASS

HOW THINGS ARE NOW

In the United States few of us know how people in other classes live. Social connectedness has been decreasing since the 1970s as income segregation in housing has separated us into economic enclaves. This has led to a lack of knowledge and understanding between/ among the classes. Programs in education, health, and workforce development that are for people in poverty are more often than not designed without their input. Thus the phrase, "If it's *about* us, *without* us, it's not *for* us."

CONTEXT

These three mental models came from the first investigations people in poverty made while Getting Ahead was being created. They were quickly picked up by Bridges trainers and became icons for the understanding we have of class issues. These distinct environments arise when there is great inequality in wealth. The hidden rules arise from these environments and deepen the impact of being raised in generational poverty, generational middle class, and generational wealth.

MENTAL MODEL FOR POVERTY

Developed by P. DeVol, 2006

MENTAL MODEL FOR MIDDLE CLASS

Developed by P. DeVol, 2006

MENTAL MODEL FOR WEALTH

Developed by R. Payne, 2005

ANALYTICAL TERMS

Mental Bandwidth	Concrete/abstract
Power	Invisible, little influence/powerful
Stability	Daily instability/long-term stability
Time Horizon	Tyranny of the moment/long view
Problem-solving Approach	Reactive problem solving with relationships/ proactive problem solving
Financial Security	Daily insecurity/long-term security

Source: Philip E. DeVol, adapted from Facilitator Notes for Getting Ahead in a Just-Gettin'-By World, 2013.

CORE IDEAS

The environments represented by the mental models explain differences in such aspects of life as driving forces, stability, power, time for abstract endeavors, time horizon, financial security, and problem-solving approaches. Poverty is experienced locally. Poverty in a Rust Belt city is different from poverty in a rural county or a prosperous, high-tech city; the barriers and opportunities will be specific to the Bridges site.

Poverty is also experienced differently by each individual according to a number of conditions and influences including race, gender, ethnicity, age, disability, sexual orientation, immigrant status, and religion.

HOW TO USE THE TOOL

- Learn about poverty in your community by engaging Getting Ahead investigators and graduates. They can share the results of their investigations into poverty as it is experienced locally, their assessment of community, and their mental model of community prosperity.

- Include Getting Ahead graduates as speakers and facilitators during Bridges workshops and events, poverty simulations, and media events. Use knowledge of the environments and hidden rules to navigate new settings more skillfully.

- Use knowledge of the environments and hidden rules to navigate social settings more skillfully.
- During meetings, establish a safe setting and process so people can speak freely about hidden rules that are broken.
- Design programs so that hidden rules that break relationships are brought to light, then eliminated.
- Provide leadership training for people in poverty who want to serve on boards.

LEARN MORE

Read *Bridges to Sustainable Communities,* Philip E. DeVol, 2010.

3. THEORY OF CHANGE

HOW THINGS ARE NOW

Problem-solving programs of any sort (workforce development, behavioral, emotional, health) require change from individuals. Change is hard, especially for those who are overwhelmed by instability and a lack of resources. Experience tells us that there are few poverty programs that are comprehensive and even fewer that share their theories of change with their subjects.

CONTEXT

The theory of change laid out in the Getting Ahead workbook puts all the cards on the table so that the Getting Ahead investigator can choose to use the change model—or not. It turns out that the Getting Ahead Theory of Change works for institutions and communities too. When they become unstable and under-resourced, they too tend to fall into the tyranny of the moment and their leaders typically seek out immediate, short term solutions when what they need is a way to break out of the tyranny of the moment.

TO ESCAPE THE TYRANNY OF THE MOMENT WE NEED

- A safe place to talk
- Time for dialogue
- Detachment and objectivity
- New information and education
- Thinking and analysis
- Plans and procedural steps
- A support team

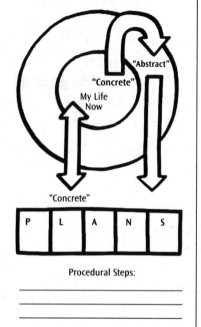

"Abstract"

"Concrete"

My Life Now

"Concrete"

P	L	A	N	S

Procedural Steps:

_____

_____

_____

Source: Philip E. DeVol, *Facilitator Notes for Getting Ahead in a Just-Gettin'-By World*, 2013.

CORE IDEAS

Those who manage Bridges initiatives must be experts in facilitating change because we ask for change at four levels: individual, institutional, community, and policy. Living in unstable environments will force people to spend time, social capital, and mental bandwidth to fix problems with cars, childcare, housing, safety, and food. Using reactive problem-solving skills and relationships, they fix problems on the fly over and over again, only to maintain themselves in poverty.

An institution or community that becomes under-resourced may lose sight of the long view and may attempt to solve problems by cutting staff, shifting costs to employees, cutting professional development costs, selling off assets, dropping research and development activities, failing to maintain infrastructure, cutting services, and increasing fees in order to survive. Leaders caught in the tyranny of the moment, or "short-termism," tend to try to solve their problems using the same thinking and solutions again and again.

Getting Ahead investigators are able to use the theory of change even when living in chaos by making a conscious choice to think in the abstract and take the long view. It helps to be in a safe place, with people who share a common language and have sufficient time to devote to the process. To break out of the tyranny of the moment one must go to the abstract, defined by the terms in the "abstract" space. Through detachment and objectivity a person can think, do an analysis that leads to finding new information, make plans, and take procedural steps that will lead to a new future story.

HOW TO USE THE TOOL

- Identify the tyranny of the moment for yourself and others.
- Find a safe place and safe people where you can find the mental bandwidth to think, to be in the abstract.
- Investigate new information.
- Think outside the box or bubble that is formed by a concrete environment.
- Guard against predators who take advantage of chaos.
- Recognize that people in institutions and communities also can get trapped in the tyranny of the moment.

LEARN MORE

Read *Facilitator Notes for Getting Ahead in a Just-Gettin'-By World*, Philip E. DeVol, 2013.

4. THREE CLASSES AT THE TABLE

HOW THINGS ARE NOW

People in poverty are very rarely at the planning and decision-making tables, even when poverty is the issue. The middle class and wealthy have normalized their role as decision makers so thoroughly that invariably they default to taking charge automatically. This entrenched rankism is sometimes seen even in Bridges initiatives.

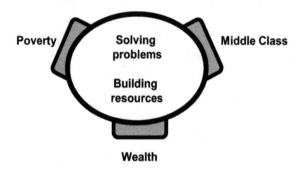

Source: Terie Dreussi-Smith, Jodi R. Pfarr, & Philip E. DeVol, Bridges Trainer Certification Manual, 2006.

CONTEXT

People in poverty have information that is vital to planning. They have concrete knowledge of the environment of poverty, the barriers that they encounter when they navigate the systems set up by institutions, and the barriers to upward mobility that exist in the community.

CORE IDEAS

Organizers seek out, invite, and listen to people in poverty. Room must be made at decision-making tables; work, decisions, and leadership must be shared. Everyone is viewed as a problem solver and a co-creator, sometimes playing the role of a coach, sometimes of a challenger. Images of "teaching a man to fish," or "giving someone a hand up" represent the hierarchical structures of class. A more fitting image would be "working shoulder to shoulder." Mike Saccocio of City Mission in Schenectady tells of the day that he was traveling with a Getting Ahead graduate to present to two New York Supreme Court judges when he realized that the roles had reversed: She was the leader, and his role was to drive her there.

Everyone around the table will benefit from examining their own experiences with class structures. And, if need be, recognize that they may have normalized and benefited from their societal status. Becoming conscious of rank and rankism can help people build healthy authentic relationships.

HOW TO USE THE TOOL

- Utilize Getting Ahead as an engagement tool. Begin engaging investigators when deciding when and where to conduct the classes. Share the work of making it a successful learning experience. Plan the graduation together and design the follow-up programs and problem-solving strategies together.
- The percentage of people from poverty at the planning table should be at least 25%.
- Provide to the people from poverty the same opportunities that you offer to anyone else to attend leadership courses, board trainings, and national conferences.

LEARN MORE

Read *From Vision to Action,* Jesse Conrad & Dan Shenk (Eds.), 2013, and *The Power of TED—The Empowerment Dynamic,* David Emerald, 2005.

5. COMMUNITY AT RISK

HOW THINGS ARE NOW

The number of cities and counties that qualify as distressed is growing; middle-class stability has been shaken; the median household income has been stagnant since the late '70s; the working class is slipping into situational poverty, using safety-net resources to stay above water; and upward mobility has stalled out for most U.S. residents.

IS YOUR COMMUNITY AT RISK?
INDICATORS OF DISTRESS

☐ Population loss

☐ Middle-class flight

☐ Young-adult children leave the community and don't come back

☐ Lost manufacturing

☐ Tax delinquencies/foreclosures

☐ More temporary and part-time jobs

☐ Rising food insecurity

☐ Low-income housing costs above 30% of income

☐ Growing number of payday lending, cash advance, pawn shops, and lease/ purchase outlets

☐ Free and reduced lunch rates rising

☐ Number and value of business loans are declining

☐ Investment in infrastructure is declining

☐ Fiscal difficulties for city or county

☐ City or county hiring freezes or layoffs

☐ Deteriorating Main Street

Source: Philip E. DeVol, *Bridges to Sustainable Communities*, 2010, and *Getting Ahead in Just-Gettin'-By World*, 2013, Module 8.

CONTEXT

Communities that use the Bridges constructs recognize that to address poverty effectively we must engage the whole community. This thinking tool is used to bring the distress level of the community to light.

CORE IDEAS

Getting Ahead investigators begin their work by naming the problems they face. This relevant and sometimes painful information acts as a motivator. It is used to create a discrepancy between what is and what could be—a future story. Bridges collaboratives can do the same by naming and facing the problems in a community.

HOW TO USE THE TOOL

- This list of risk factors in this thinking tool is to be used to spark conversation and investigation. The community bank in Martinsville, Indiana, recognized the connection between distress factors in the community and poverty and was the catalyst for Bridges in its community and beyond.

- Utilize information generated by Getting Ahead investigators during the class: the Mental Models of Poverty, Community Assessment, and the Mental Model of Community Prosperity.

- Use Module 8 of Getting Ahead to assess the community.

LEARN MORE

Read *Bridges to Sustainable Communities,* Philip E. DeVol, 2010.

6. BRIDGES STEERING COMMITTEES

HOW THINGS ARE NOW

There are many things that make it difficult for a community to collaborate. Here's a short list: silos and funding streams that support them, competing agendas/problems/initiatives, partners that come and go as leaders change jobs, short-term planning and goals, differing perceptions regarding the problems, and a lack of common language and metrics.

DEVELOPING A BRIDGES COMMUNITY
Purpose and Function of a BRIDGES STEERING COMMITTEE

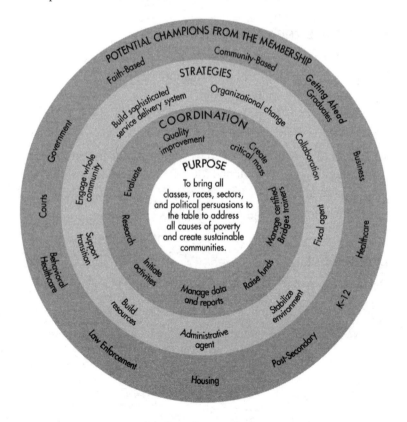

Source: Philip E. DeVol, *Bridges to Sustainable Communities*, 2010.

CONTEXT

Bridges provides a common language, core constructs, and tools that will help overcome the barriers listed above. Because poverty impacts all sectors (schools, health, criminal justice, employment, and so on), it is possible for every sector to achieve its goals while participating in a collaborative. In addition, Bridges is not a program, so its concepts can support other national or sector initiatives, such as Opportunity Nation, Healthy Communities, or Strive. In that sense Bridges is an additive that can enhance any initiative.

CORE IDEAS

It is in communities where we can have the greatest impact. It is where we have connections, local knowledge, influence, and, above all, a reason to act. It is, after all, where we live. This tool is descriptive, not prescriptive. It helps conceptualize the work of a Bridges Steering Committee.

HOW TO USE THE TOOL

- Communities find their own names for the groups they form—e.g., Marion Matters or Stillwater Cares.
- The "coordination" ring represents the work done by the institution or collaboratives that act in the role of catalyst, sponsor, administrative, and fiscal agent. In some communities the coordination role is shared by two or more organizations according to who the fiscal agent is for a grant or by sharing supportive services. Some communities, such as St. Joseph County (Indiana) Bridges Out of Poverty Initiative, formed a nonprofit that has paid staff, interns, AmeriCorps personnel, and volunteers managing the work under a board of directors. The membership is made up of 40-plus organizations.
- The "membership strategies" ring names some of the actions taken by organizations that are embedding Bridges concepts in their work.

- Communities will often generate champions who use Bridges so successfully that other organizations in the community and beyond seek them out as models.
- The "thinking tools" are designed to enhance the work of Bridges Steering Committees.

LEARN MORE

Read *Bridges to Sustainable Communities,* Philip E. DeVol, 2010, Chapters 3, 5 (which contains the chart above), and 6.

7. COMMUNITY SUSTAINABILITY GRID

HOW THINGS ARE NOW

As long as our communities (and nation) are confused about the causes of poverty, our strategies to address poverty will be confused. We will be subject to the "either/ or" thinking promoted by talk radio, newspapers, cable television, magazines, and think tanks with political agendas. This environment makes it difficult to hold a true dialogue about the problems and to take meaningful action at the community and national level.

COMMUNITY SUSTAINABILITY GRID
A COMPREHENSIVE PLANNING TOOL FOR BRIDGES STEERING COMMITTEES

Name the Barrier	Individual Behavior	Human and Social Capital in the Community	Exploitation	Political/Economic Structures
Individual Action				
Organizational Action				
Community Action				
Policy				

ADDRESS ALL CAUSES OF POVERTY

Source: Philip E. DeVol, *Getting Ahead in a Just-Gettin'-By World,* 2013.

CONTEXT

The Community Sustainability Grid is based on the Research Continuum that organizes research topics into four clusters: individual choice and behavior, conditions in the community, exploitation, and political/economic structures. The grid is designed to help a Bridges initiative address all the causes.

CORE IDEAS

There is good research in all four clusters. This means that Bridges initiatives can offer their communities a "both/and" approach to poverty that will attract people from all political persuasions. In other words, poverty is caused both by individual choices and behaviors and political/economic structures and everything in between, such as community conditions and exploitation.

HOW TO USE THE TOOL

- Identify issues to work on by listening to Getting Ahead graduates. They have the most relevant information on the barriers.
- Use the form to address one barrier or problem at a time.
- Name the barrier in the top left-hand cell in the table.
- Be as thorough as possible when brainstorming and selecting solutions one row at a time.
- Name the specific solution or action step, as well as the responsible person or organization.

LEARN MORE

For an example of a grid that has been filled in, go to the *Getting Ahead* workbook, 2013, pages 220–224.

8. BRIDGES CONTINUUM

HOW THINGS ARE NOW

In our communities today most people are looking to someone else to solve the poverty problem. We tend to look first to the individuals in poverty and the organizations that encounter and serve them ("If only (fill in the blank) would (fill in the blank) then (fill in the blank) "). Some communities recognize the connection between high poverty rates and community sustainability more quickly than others. The tipping point for some of the more stable communities is when the free- and reduced-lunch rate climbs above 40%. For more distressed communities, however, 40% would be considered an unrealistic goal.

THE BRIDGES CONTINUUM
A COMPREHENSIVE PLANNING TOOL FOR BRIDGES STEERING COMMITTEES

	Preconception to 6	K—12	Post-Secondary	Workforce Placement	Job Retention	Self-Sufficient Wage	Seniors	Wellness	Community Prosperity
Metrics									
Fallout Costs									
Bridges Strategies									
Responsible for Action									

ADDRESS POVERTY AT EVERY STEP OF LIFE

Source: Philip E. DeVol & Scott Miller, *Facilitator Notes for Getting Ahead in a Just-Gettin'-By World*, 2013.

CONTEXT

Bridges Communities are the exception to this. Instead of looking to others to address poverty, they take responsibility across multiple sectors. The growth of Bridges initiatives tends to move organically from one or two organizations that use Bridges to the collective realization that collaboration will be more effective and cost-efficient.

CORE IDEAS

Rather than waiting on federal or state policies to change Bridges initiatives, capitalize on local connections and influence to take action.

This tool features these concepts:
- Poverty can be addressed at every stage of life.
- Almost every sector can participate in stabilizing the environment and building resources.
- Community metrics must be identified to set reasonable goals and to serve the purpose of each organization.
- Some people are drawn to Bridges by their hearts, others by their heads. Those drawn by their heads need to see numbers. Poverty is costly; it's not a good economic model.
- Identify the solutions offered by aha! Process and the Bridges Community of Practice.
- Successful approaches in one sector can often be adapted to improve outcomes in another sector. For example, employers have created strategies to improve retention rates. These strategies can then be adapted and used by colleges and universities to improve their graduation rates of under-resourced students.
- This tool illustrates how most organizations can be responsible for doing something to address poverty.
- Bridges can prevent poverty, alleviate suffering, and support people in transition.

HOW TO USE THE TOOL

- Share this tool at all trainings; it will help people see how they can fit into the Bridges work.
- Attract people in all sectors.
- Illustrate what each sector can do and how it will benefit by joining the initiative.
- Illustrate the need for collaboration.
- Create a local version of this table.

LEARN MORE

Read *Bridges to Sustainable Communities,* Philip E. DeVol, 2010, and *Facilitator Notes for Getting Ahead in a Just-Gettin'-By World,* Philip E. DeVol, 2013.

9. 'GETTING BY' RESOURCES VS. 'GETTING AHEAD' RESOURCES

HOW THINGS ARE NOW

How poverty is defined points to what the solution is expected to be. So in the U.S. the definition is based on income, so the solution must be to increase one's income. This simplistic definition of poverty cannot address the complex causes of poverty, the lack of social coherence, or the balance between a safety net and opportunities for upward mobility. The current approach has devolved into cliff effects that destabilize people just when they most need stability. And many programs have fallen into a pattern of providing people with just enough resources to maintain them in poverty, including individuals who have one or more minimum-wage jobs.

	Financial	Emotional	Mental	Spiritual	Physical	Support Systems	Relationships/ Role Models	Knowledge of Hidden Rules	Integrity and Trust	Motivation and Persistence	Formal Register
'Getting By' Resources											
'Getting Ahead' Resources											

Adapted from J. Pfarr Consulting

CONTEXT

In Bridges, poverty is defined as the extent to which individuals, institutions, and communities do without resources. That concept gives everyone something to do about poverty: build resources. This tool deepens our understanding of the 11 resources by giving communities a way to think and talk about the balance between a safety net and a support system for making the transition out of poverty.

CORE IDEAS

Distinguishing between "getting by" resources and "getting ahead" resources can be difficult. For example, one woman had to choose between taking a better-paying job and losing her subsidized housing. The subsidized housing, which provided much-needed stability, was a disincentive for change. She said, "It's scary to step from a shaky safety net to a shaky ladder. Who knows if the job will be there next year?"

Institutions and funders need to determine if they are merely bringing resources to people on the one hand or helping them build resources on the other. All of these decisions come together as a piece that determines whether or not someone can make the climb out of poverty. Communities that offer Getting Ahead must make a commitment to support people in poverty during that long, hard climb.

HOW TO USE THE TOOL

- Individuals analyze their resources during Getting Ahead classes.
- Institutions can analyze the resources they provide. St. Vincent de Paul, a national faith-based organization that has a long history of working directly with the poor, is using this tool to rebalance its approach.
- Community collaboratives can use the tool to review resource utilization and opportunities. A number of food

banks are thinking how they can "shorten the line" by addressing root causes of food insecurity.

- Funders are particularly interested in initiative-based approaches rather than needs-based funding. They have the flexibility to change how funding is allocated in ways that most fixed federal and state programs don't.

- Use this tool to open a discussion on funding patterns. Much of the funding for poverty is designed to help people manage poverty. Those organizations often resist initiative-based funding because it threatens their funding stream and their staff. Finding innovative ways to shift some funds to support people who are moving out of poverty is a current debate. This thinking tool feeds that conversation at the local, state, and national levels.

LEARN MORE

Read *Bridges Certified Trainer Manual—Institutional and Community Lenses, 2014.*

10. METHODOLOGY: INNOVATION

HOW THINGS ARE NOW

Top-down models of knowledge transfer often prescribe programs that require compliance. They are not always open to innovation and are less likely to be sustainable because local adopters have taken little ownership of the concepts.

CONTEXT

As noted, Bridges is not a program but a set of shared constructs that can be applied in many ways. These concepts, books, and trainings come from Bridges consultants and aha! Process, Inc. People are first attracted to the concepts. But they also are attracted to the Bridges methodology, which is that individuals, institutions, and communities are encouraged to "own" the concepts, to see themselves as co-creators, and to invent new programs and strategies.

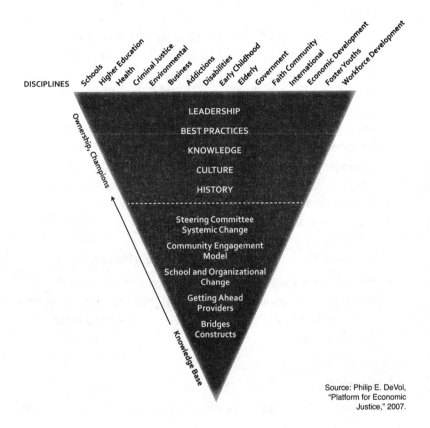

Source: Philip E. DeVol, "Platform for Economic Justice," 2007.

CORE IDEAS

In Bridges everyone, starting with people in poverty, is viewed as problem solvers. The co-creator concept includes those around the coffeepot at particular agencies, people in the community who are also using Bridges, people from particular sectors, Bridges sites from around the country, and Bridges consultants. This natural learning process has generated a network of Bridges sites out of which has come Advancing Bridges, Inc., an independent non-profit with the mission of building the Bridges movement.

HOW TO USE THE TOOL

- Bridges provides the basic concepts and some programs that appear under the dotted line in the mental model above.

- Those who apply the concepts naturally take into account the history, culture, knowledge base, leadership, and best practices of their organization, community, or discipline. Judge Carol Robb, Columbiana County (Ohio) Municipal Court, made nine policy changes in her court that not only saved the county money but helped stabilize the lives of the offenders. The simplest change was to switch from specific appointment times for offenders to see the probation officer to setting a day and time by which the meeting with the probation officer must take place. This saved the county the cost of issuing bench warrants and stabilized the lives of offenders by not needing to send them to jail. Several courts in Ohio and beyond have also adopted this strategy.

- The solutions that arise from this methodology will then be relevant and sustainable. Adopting this thinking tool can open the door to the expansion of Bridges into many more disciplines or sectors.

LEARN MORE

Read blog: "What Makes Getting Ahead and Bridges Work?" Philip E. DeVol, 2014.

11. CYCLE OF INNOVATION:
KNOWLEDGE AND TECHNOLOGY

HOW THINGS ARE NOW

Bridges sites may be creating new solutions and not have the intention or capacity to share their new ideas with others. During the process of building a Bridges initiative, individuals, organizations, and communities move along the learning continuum from novice to expert. In a learning community of so many sites, sectors, and communities, movement from novice, beginner, competent, proficient, and expert is uneven. In addition, the Bridges Community of Practice has not been formalized.

Source: Jodi R. Pfarr, *Bridges Trainer Certification Manual*, 2007.

CONTEXT

aha! Process provides books, trainings, and consulting. In addition, it offers the learning community quarterly teleconferences for various sectors; websites; blogs; webinars; newsletters; an annual conference; and *From Vision to Action,* a publication of best practices. As the knowledge base grows, so does the demand for a systemic approach to managing and spreading new information.

CORE IDEAS

Breakthrough innovations can occur at any time. When they do, technology can be used to spread the information from individuals to institutions and communities. Evidence must be collected and reported to ensure growth. The marriage of innovations and technology seems self-evident when looking at the rapid growth of new products in the digital world, but for people working on poverty issues, it is more remote. A structure and technology tools are needed to capture and share new, sometimes brilliant, ideas.

HOW TO USE THE TOOL

- This thinking tool is designed to illustrate the random way in which brilliant breakthroughs can occur and how technology can move the new information from the individual to the community.

- It's also designed to help communities establish an intention to participate in the cycle of innovation to become champion sites that others seek out. Cascade Engineering, a plastics firm in Michigan, was the first Bridges champion by creating an approach that improved its retention rate of under-resourced workers dramatically. Cascade's breakthrough has led to more breakthroughs in the business sector.

- Bridges sites need to begin with the end in mind—that is to say, decide on a data-gathering evaluation tool and invest in technology.

- Establish a historian—someone to document the progress, identify the innovations and Bridges concepts that sparked them, maintain a database of those trained in Bridges and Getting Ahead, and celebrate the results.

- Individual organizations can investigate the use of MPOWR's cloud-based data management and reporting system. The full package collects data on the development of the 11 resources for Getting Ahead graduates, 15 life areas, individual case planning, and case management. MPOWR also has a Getting Ahead Module that provides data about development of the 11 resources.

- Community collaboratives can investigate the use of MPOWR across several organizations, thus creating a single plan for GA grads or clients rather than having a plan at every organization. This provides common outcomes for all collaborative members—and access to national data from Bridges sites.

LEARN MORE

Read *The Wisdom of Crowds,* James Surowiecki, 2005.

12. BRIDGES COMMUNITIES OF PRACTICE MODEL

HOW THINGS ARE NOW

Even though learning communities are a natural and organic way of learning, they are difficult to support when the members are from many states and sectors—and seven countries! In addition, champion sites can be overwhelmed by the number of calls they field from new Bridges sites. While the basic technology for a web-based learning community exists, the maintenance of this learning and knowledge transfer model is still relatively new and does not include all sites.

Source: Terie Dreussi-Smith, Jodi R. Pfarr, & Philip E. DeVol,
Bridges Trainer Certification Manual, 2006.

CONTEXT

aha! Process conducts webinars, publishes books, issues newsletters, and hosts an annual conference.

In 2013 the nonprofit organization Advancing Bridges was formed to promote and support the Bridges movement, adding another link in the learning community.

CORE IDEAS

Members of the Bridges Community of Practice include individual Bridges sites, city or countywide Bridges collaboratives, statewide Bridges initiatives, and sector communities of practice (criminal justice, employers, post-secondary, Getting Ahead, health/healthcare, etc.). The lines that link the communities of practice are both formal and informal. The knowledge base is expanding and becoming more effective at sharing information and supporting new initiatives.

HOW TO USE THE TOOL

- Be intentional about participating in the Bridges Community of Practice.
- Assign board members to attend community of practice teleconferences so they can report back on the latest information coming from such sectors as criminal justice, post-secondary, health/healthcare, reentry, and employer/workforce.
- Participate in multiple-site program development.
- Share best practices and outcomes through publications and websites, as well as at national conferences.

LEARN MORE

Read *Cultivating Communities of Practice: A Guide to Managing Knowledge,* Etienne Wenger, Richard McDermott, & William M. Snyder, 2002.

CONCLUSION

Utilizing these 12 thinking tools is a form of participatory action research. People involved in Bridges initiatives learn through their investigations and the innovative ideas they put into action, using the growth of their knowledge to feed the cycle of learning. This means that individuals, organizations, and communities can benefit by applying Bridges concepts even while they are contributing to the next cycle of learning and a deeper level of impact.

Bridges has been called a movement because it grows naturally, as if on its own. People want to join because they can see that good things will happen. It is a social movement that inspires people to work together and in so doing build social capital; it is an economic movement because its purpose is to bring stability, security, and a higher quality of life. Bridges isn't a political movement, even though it must eventually influence policymakers.

Political/economic promoters offer "narratives" or a story line that presents their explanation of the past and their version of what the future might be and pit one group against another. The Bridges narrative is free of, and broader than, existing narratives because it isn't bound by the absolutes of competing economic and political ideologies. It's a safe place in the center of the community where sensible, non-partisan dialogue guides action.

Two recent studies confirm that there is middle ground where reasonable people can meet to solve community problems. The studies point to what we in Bridges have already found to be true; conservatives and progressives largely agree on many key aspects about poverty. There are Bridges sites in communities known to be very conservative and in communities that are regarded as very progressive or liberal. And we know they are all using Bridges concepts to take action on the serious problems of poverty and community sustainability.

The McClatchy-Marist National Poll survey of 1,197 adults was conducted between February 4 and 9, 2014. The other recent poll was designed and conducted by the Half in Ten Campaign and the Center for American Progress; it was released in January 2014.

The McClatchy-Marist poll shows that Democrats, Independents, and Republicans largely agreed that it takes even more effort to get ahead in the United States these days than in previous generations. Their responses to the question about "more effort":

Strong Democrats	85%
Soft Democrats	77%
Just Independents	82%
Soft Republicans	77%
Strong Republicans	82%

To the question, "In this country right now, do you think people who work hard have a good chance of improving their standard of living" or "still have a hard time maintaining their standard of living," people from all three groups largely agreed that "people still have a hard time maintaining their standard of living."

Strong Democrats	72%
Soft Democrats	72%
Just Independents	75%
Soft Republicans	65%
Strong Republicans	58%

The findings from "50 Years After LBJ's War on Poverty: A Study of American Attitudes About Work, Economic Opportunity, and the Social Safety Net" done by the Center for American Progress, in cooperation with the Half in Ten Campaign, address the attitudes people have about individuals in poverty.

To the question, "Do you agree or disagree: 'Most people living in poverty are decent people who are working hard to make ends meet in a difficult economy'?" Most people agreed with the statement.

Millennials	82%
African Americans	92%
Latinos	82%
White liberals/progressives	92%
White moderates	76%
White conservatives/libertarians	66%

To the question, "Do you agree or disagree: 'The primary reason so many people are living in poverty today is that our economy is failing to produce enough jobs that pay decent wages'?" Most people agreed with the statement:

Millennials	77%
African Americans	78%
Latinos	80%
White liberals/progressives	79%
White moderates	80%
White conservatives/libertarians	76%

There is every reason for Bridges Communities to take hope and energy from these findings, as well as from their own experience working with people across class and political lines. It is increasingly urgent that we become ever more effective because, frankly, it isn't likely that the global economy will suddenly change course and start promoting stable workplace environments and more opportunities to build resources. The healthiest response in these difficult times is to work in our own communities, document our success, and create a narrative—a future story—that others also can benefit from and put into practice.

GLOSSARY

Bridges Out of Poverty: the title of the book that has been shortened to "Bridges" when referring to concepts, initiatives, and communities.

Bridges Community: a place where there is a Bridges Steering Committee.

Bridges initiative: a program or approach that is based on Bridges and conducted by a single organization or collaborative.

Bridges Steering Committee: the people from various organizations who are using Bridges concepts and meet regularly to collaborate and expand the work.

Common language: shared information on environments of class, causes of poverty, hidden rules of class, language issues, resources, etc.

Community of Practice: a structured approach for people within a discipline or movement who intend to document and improve their practices.

Getting Ahead: referring to the workbook and accompanying facilitator notes, *Getting Ahead in a Just-Gettin'-By World.*

Getting Ahead: referring to the program in which people from poverty graduate after taking a 12-week course.

Hidden rules: the unspoken cues and habits of a group that arise from their environment.

Learning community: a group that learns together with activities and intention but not as a formal Community of Practice.

Mental models: stories, metaphors, parables, videos, and two-dimensional drawings that represent complex abstract ideas. Also an internal picture or world view.

MPOWR: a cloud-based data collection and evaluation tool provided by SupplyCore, Inc.

Resources: Ruby Payne's definition of poverty is "the extent to which an individual does without resources": financial, mental, social/support systems, emotional, physical, spiritual, language/formal register, motivation and persistence, integrity and trust, relationships/role models, knowledge of hidden rules.

IN CLOSING

Poverty is still with us because our collective mindset has allowed it to exist and because it's very hard to get out of poverty, particularly at this time in U.S. history. The work already being done by Bridges Communities can inspire us to form the intention to do more to help individuals and families out of poverty and to help our communities become prosperous. The ideas expressed in these papers are part of a growing body of knowledge and a growing community of practice. The credit for the many positive things that have been done—and will be done—lies with the people who have taken ownership of Bridges and are now creating new strategies, relationships, and tools. My thanks to all of you.

ENDNOTES

[i] Parrott, Sharon. (November 24, 2008). Center on Budget and Policy Priorities. Washington, DC. "Recession Could Cause Large Increases in Poverty and Push Millions into Deep Poverty: Stimulus Package Should Include Polices to Ameliorate Harshest Effects of Downturn."

[ii] http://www.wfco.org/RenderLobbies. aspx?lobbyId=72&mid=59&mmid=2.

[iii] Informal surveys of *Bridges* workshop audiences done by *Bridges* consultants report that clients from poverty are going to three to nine agencies a year to get their concrete needs met.

[iv] Hawken, Paul, Lovins, Amory, & Lovins, L. H. (1999). *Natural Capitalism: Creating the Next Industrial Revolution.* Boston, MA: Little, Brown and Company.

[v] Ibid.

[vi] Ibid.

[vii] www.usenews.com/usnews/biztech/tools/modebtratio.htm.

[viii] Andrews, Edmund L. (2009). *Busted: Life Inside the Great Mortgage Meltdown.* New York, NY: W. W. Norton.

[ix] Sapolsky, Robert M. (1998). *Why Zebras Don't Get Ulcers: An Updated Guide to Stress, Stress-Related Diseases, and Coping.* New York, NY: W. H. Freeman and Company.

[x] Sered, Susan Starr, & Fernandopulle, Rushika. (2005). *Uninsured In America: Life and Death in the Land of Opportunity.* Berkeley, CA: University of California Press.

[xi] Schwartz, Peter. (1996). *The Art of the Long View: Planning for the Future in an Uncertain World.* New York, NY: Currency Doubleday, p. 231.

[xii] World Bank. (2005). *World Development Report 2006: Equity and Development.* New York, NY: Oxford University Press.

[xiii] Hart, Betty, and Risley, Todd R. (1995). *Meaningful Differences in the Everyday Experience of Young American Children.* Baltimore, MD: Paul H. Brookes Publishing Co.

[xiv] www.web.intuit.com/about_intuit/press_releases/2000/01-04.htm.

[xv] http://www.washingtonpost.com/wp-srv/politics/documents/american_journal_of_medicine_09.pdf. Medical Bankruptcy in the United States, 2007: Results of a National Study. (2009). *The American Journal of Medicine.*

[xvi] Miller, Matthew. (2009). *The Tyranny of Dead Ideas: Letting Go of the Old Ways of Thinking to Unleash a New Prosperity.* New York, NY: Times Books.

[xvii] Putnam, Robert D. (2000). *Bowling Alone: the Collapse and Revival of American Community.* New York, NY: Simon & Schuster.

[xviii] www.sos.state.oh.us

■ ■ ■ ■

More eye-openers at ...
www.ahaprocess.com

Visit www.ahaprocess.com for free resources: our free webinars, articles, video clips, success stories, and read our blog!

Sign up for our latest workshop offerings (many online), including:

- Getting Ahead while Getting Out Facilitator Certification
- Getting Ahead in a Just-Gettin'-By World Facilitator Training
- Bridges to Health and Healthcare
- Applying Bridges Concepts: Individual and Institutional
- Bridges Out of Poverty Trainer Certification
- Building a Sustainable Community
- Understanding Class for First Responders

Visit www.gettingaheadnetwork.com for more information on community-based models that will work where you live

If you like Bridges to *Sustainable Communities*, check out:

- *Bridges to Health and Healthcare: New solutions for improving access and services* (Payne, Dreussi-Smith, Shaw, & Young)
- *From Vision to Action, Vol. II: Best Practices to reduce the impact of poverty in communities, education, healthcare, and more* (peer-reviewed articles written by practitioners of the work)
- *Investigations into Economic Class in America & Facilitator Notes* (DeVol & Krodel). This is Getting Ahead adapted for college students
- *Getting Ahead while Getting Out: A prisoner reentry model to reduce recidivism through learning, building resources, accountability, and collaboration* (DeVol)
- *Tactical Communication: Mastering effective interactions with citizens of diverse backgrounds* (Pfarr)

Connect with us on FaceBook, Twitter, and Pinterest, and watch our YouTube channel

For a complete listing of products please visit www.ahaprocess.com